COMMUNICATING IN CRISIS

COMMUNICATING IN CRISIS

Michel Ogrizek
Jean-Michel Guillery

Translated by
Helen Kimball-Brooke and Robert Z. Brooke

ALDINE DE GRUYTER

New York

ABOUT THE AUTHORS

Michel Ogrizek directs corporate relations worldwide for the Unilever group. A medical doctor by training with a background in social and cultural anthropology and wide-ranging experience in public health, he has published several books on communication. This is his first book in English.

Jean-Michel Guillery is a medical doctor and a former journalist. He has specialized as an expert consultant in the prevention and handling of commercial and industrial risks, in the fields of health, nuclear, petroleum and farm produce industries. He has developed an original methodology for training programmes and crisis simulation scenarios.

Originally published as *La communication de crise*
© Presses Universitaires de France, 1997

ALDINE DE GRUYTER
A division of Walter de Gruyter, Inc.
200 Saw Mill River Road
Hawthorne, New York 10532

This publication is printed on acid free paper ∞

Library of Congress Cataloging-in-Publication Data
Ogrizek, Michel.
    [Communication de crise.   English]
    Communicating in crisis : a theoretical and practical guide to crisis management / Michel Ogrizek and Jean-Michel Guillery ; translated by Helen C. Kimball-Brooke and Robert Z. Brooke.
        p.   cm.
    Includes bibliographical references.
    ISBN 0-202-30632-1 (pbk. alk. paper)
    1. Crisis management.   2. Communication in management.
I. Guillery, Jean-Michel.   II. Title.
HD49.03613   1999
658.4'056—dc21   99-30182
                                                        CIP

Manufactured in the United States of America

10 9 8 7 6 5 4 3 2 1

CONTENTS

FOREWORD
Stephen A. Greyser ix

INTRODUCTION
What Is Crisis Communication? xi

1   PRODUCT RISK AND CRISIS
    COMMUNICATION 1

        I.   Rumors 1
        II.   Product Contamination 6
        III.   Accidents 17
        IV.   Boycotts 21
        V.   New Risks and New Product Crises 25

2   INDUSTRIAL RISK AND
    CRISIS COMMUNICATION 29

        I.   Major Technological Accidents 29
        II.   Setting Up or Expanding an Industrial Site 33
        III.   Industrial Waste Management 36

3   INSTITUTIONAL RISK AND
    CRISIS COMMUNICATION 37

        I.   Corporate Identity Crises 38
        II.   Media/Legal Crises and Scandals 39
        III.   Industrial Restructuring 40

IV.   Financial Communication in
      Times of Crisis 44
V.   Internal Crisis Communication 45

4 MAJOR COLLECTIVE FEARS AND
   CRISIS COMMUNICATION 47

   I.   Terrorism 48
   II. Major Health Fears 50

5 COMMUNICATING IN A CRISIS 53

   I.   Major Principles 53
   II.   Developing Scenarios 58
   III. Communicating with the Victims 60
   IV.   Internal Communication First 64
   V.   Crisis Communication and the Media 65
   VI.   Symbolic Communication 67

6 CRISIS UNIT ORGANIZATION
   AND OPERATION 73

   I.   Unit Organization 73
   II.   Unit Members and Their Roles 76
   III. Working Methods 78
   IV.   Managing the Postcrisis Period 80

7 TRAINING AND PREPARING FOR
   CRISIS COMMUNICATION 85

   I.   Case Studies 85
   II.   Setting Up a Crisis Unit 86
   III. Simulation Exercises 87
   IV.   Preparing for Crisis Prevention
         and Avoidance 88

CONCLUSION 91

REFERENCES 93

FOREWORD

Corporate crises have become commonplace. Airplane crashes, oil spills, automobile safety problems, and tragedies caused by foods or drugs may be unpredictable as to time and place, but they are virtually certain to occur at some juncture.

All can have short-term negative effects on a company's reputation, and some can have long-standing effects of negative association. The tenth anniversary of the March 1989 Exxon Valdez disaster is instructive as to the staying power of the linkage of a crisis to the company involved.

An essential element in a company's efforts to cope with a crisis is communication. Effective communications are a key factor in helping to mitigate the effects of a crisis, although the underlying corporate behavior associated with the cause and/or remediation of the crisis is the foundation on which communications are able to work.

Communicating in crisis is at the core of this book. Managing in crisis, however, is the broader setting in which the communications take place. The authors provide structures for analyzing and understanding the character of different kinds of crisis situations, and for planning actions—and communications—to address them. They describe a wide variety of typical crisis situations, from rumors and boycotts to product contamination, health scares, and accidents.

They refer to a variety of specific actual cases, some in considerable detail (such as the classic Perrier situation). Here the authors spell out their views of lessons learned from the experiences.

Today's companies have a far larger landscape of prospective vulnerabilities than in the past. Some of these derive from changes in social values (e.g., environmental issues, sexual harassment), some from changes in economic structure (privatization). The authors explore how these shifts can lead to crises enmeshing entire firms.

At the same time, the extent of media coverage of business has multiplied in terms of outlets and time/space of coverage; the speed of that coverage has accelerated as well. Both create a need for companies to be alert and prepared organizationally so as to detect and address potential crises, and to respond to pressures from media and affected stakeholders.

In terms of communicating in crisis, the authors spell out a variety of key principles drawn from experiences on both sides of the Atlantic. At the same time, they caution that the speed of action required in a real crisis inhibits perfection. The principles and detailed suggested applications—including "what if" and "what next" scenarios—provide a template of preparation for communications executives and top management. This encompasses bold internal and external communications, including dealing with the media.

As noted above, companies must be organizationally prepared for crises; otherwise they will be "scrambling" and have limited opportunity for proactive initiatives and communications. In this regard, the authors are particularly helpful in describing the operational aspects of a crisis unit, including the support systems for preparedness and the roles of key unit members. They also show how preparing to manage a crisis should be accompanied by preparing to prevent and avoid one.

Crises obviously call for communications. At root, however, crisis communications are part of crisis management. In offering their analyses, philosophies, and approaches, the authors present helpful guides to enhancing management's ability to curtail and confront crisis situations.

Stephen A. Greyser
Richard P. Chapman Professor
Marketing/Communications
Harvard Business School

Introduction
What Is Crisis Communication?

Before attempting to define crisis communication, it is vital, in this day and age, to establish what it is not. First of all, it has nothing to do with gurus. The early nineties trend in which a few individuals managed to persuade everyone that corporate communication in times of crisis depended entirely on their personal skill and ability in conjuring up media tricks has unfortunately not faded away. Second, it is not a collection of secret recipes, shared by only a select few, for manipulating crisis situations to inadmissible ends.

In the minds of the public, even if now a less naive public, the very purpose of crisis communication is unfortunately still surrounded by confusion, despite the fact that the experts have gradually managed to clarify the scope and details of its application. Granted, the subject is not easy to define since crisis management and crisis communication are very tightly interwoven. In addition, the complex nature of a crisis process includes, to a certain extent, corporate communication itself. As Joseph Scanlon (1975) quite rightly emphasizes: "Every crisis is also a crisis of information. . . . Failure to control this crisis of information results in failure to control the crisis, including its directly operational aspects" (see also Scanlon 1982).

Communication in times of crisis, or *crisis communication,* consists basically of a set of concepts, principles, analysis, and working methods that apply specifically to the very particular situation known as a crisis. These concepts, principles, analysis, and methods are rooted in the diverse but—for those familiar with them—closely related human sciences of social anthropology, psychology, and *cindynics* (technological risk monitoring and management), as well as in the field of medical emergencies and disasters. Operationally, they are justified by the fact that their appropriateness and effectiveness are demonstrated *on the ground* from crisis to crisis. This notion of validation by experience is essential.

When it comes to the scope of crisis communication, the core of the matter is clearly the salient event that constitutes or marks the breakout of the crisis: a serious accident; the public revelation of a major risk; media focus on a product, a manufacturing site, or a company; open or implied denunciation of unethical practices, and so on. At times like this, when gravity takes hold or time speeds up, we know that for the institutions involved, both internal and external information and communication also become emergencies and challenges, because they may generate extra stress, indignation, or doubt, on their own, which only intensifies the crisis. This is when the analysis, concepts, principles, and methods mentioned above will help, insofar as is possible, to avoid making crude errors of judgment and prevent any worsening of the situation caused by stress-inducing delays, inappropriate reactions, or irresponsible comments.

The scope of crisis communication is not, however, limited to the few hours or days when the crisis breaks out. In most cases, if upstream methods are deployed, it can be possible to anticipate a crisis, take heed, prepare for, and even sometimes prevent the worst. A number of principles and techniques have proven to be effective on this slippery slope of identifying and managing potential crises in advance. Similarly, downstream, in the so-called postcrisis period (which in fact is part of the crisis itself, since the crisis, as we shall see, is an "open information system"), the use of specific communication methods is recommended to avoid prolonging the crisis, stimulating it, or even triggering a relapse.

I. THE CONCEPT OF CRISIS: DEFINITION-SPECIFIC CRITERIA

According to William Dab (1993), *crisis is originally a medical idea,* a Hippocratic concept. "All illnesses reach a turning point which is a state of crisis. From here, some are fatal, some go on to recovery; all others develop to another form and take on a different constitution." Crisis is therefore defined as "a fit of uncertainty and distress where everything is in suspense . . . in anticipation of imminent resolution of the illness" (Bolzinger 1982), a sort of moment of truth and choice, the point where everything changes fast and irreversibly.

This nexus of uncertainty, distress, and acceleration stands out instantly as characteristic. At a time when almost anything and everything is called a crisis, the identification, i.e., recognition and diagnosis, of a crisis, has become a problem in itself. Although crisis is not a precise concept (quite the contrary, as a concept it is vague), it is important to understand its specificity to distinguish between a crisis and other situations that might be close but whose management would be significantly different.

What then is the definition of a crisis, compared with emergencies, major risks, and disasters, knowing that governments and industrial corporations today are regularly confronted with situations whose impact on the safety and health of their populations is a major challenge?

An *emergency* can be distinguished by the unexpected outburst of a threat to a population, whether real or only possible, but in any case one that demands a rapid response. The emergency is of a disastrous kind when there is "an imbalance between needs and available resources" (WHO).

In actual *disasters,* the concept of possibility has disappeared. The reality, fact, and scale of human injury and/or natural damage make themselves felt in tragic proportions. There are times when an established disaster can generate a crisis as a secondary state. Initially, however, a disaster is clearly different from a crisis. "A disaster offers the popular imagination *the certainty that the situation is serious* according to *the terrible law of all or nothing. . . .* In contrast, a crisis tends rather to generate doubt and suspicion about reality and the advent of danger." Also, "disaster fits into the framework of a statistical vision of the risks which are the modern interpretation of destiny and divine ordeal. A crisis develops as part of a painful doubting of human risk management and our ability to control our individual or collective history" (Ogrizek 1993).

The concept of *major risk,* on the other hand, has been established by Patrick Lagadec's work (1982) on major technological risks. As William Dab (1993) puts it, the features of major risks may be summarized as:

—Extent, i.e., scale and seriousness more than frequency (the probability of occurrence is generally low).
—Invisibility and high emotional connotations.
—Major uncertainty regarding impact, with wide divergence in points of view.
—The population's inability to accept the situation, which arises particularly when such risks result from involuntary individual exposure which could have been avoided.
—Major economic challenges.
—Extensive media coverage.

Major risks demand understandably to be identified, as soon and as precisely as possible. There is a high degree of probability that they may develop into a crisis.

The difficulty in pinning down the concept of crisis has led over the last twenty years to increasing and often apposite commentary.

Crisis is confusion, a trial, a break, an opportunity. All of this is true.

Edgar Morin (1976) makes the subtle statement "Crisis means indecision. It is the moment when uncertainty looms at the same time as disruption" and concludes that "crisis point in the concept of crisis is the beginning of crisis theory."

In 1984, leaving the realm of theory, P. Lagadec offered a working definition of crisis that is still today the best foundation on which to base discussion. Although it is incomplete, it summarizes the essential aspects clearly and most relevantly: "Crisis: a situation in which numerous organizations are faced with critical problems, experience both sharp external pressure and bitter internal tensions, and are then brutally and for an extended period thrust to centre stage and hurled one against the other . . . all in a society of mass communication, in other words in direct contact, with the certainty of being at the top of the news on radio and television and in the press for a long time."

Component parts of this definition that should be stressed are the importance of the media, the length of the crisis, and the idea—often actually key—of internal tension. Over subsequent years, P. Lagadec (1981, 1982, 1993a, 1993b, 1990, 1995) managed to go further in characterizing crises with his five different states of crisis: outbreak and its corollary, overflow; disorder; loss of credibility; divergence of many kinds; and destabilization. Extensive experience in crisis management shows that these successive waves build up and then break. This is true for all types of crisis: industrial, institutional, social, political, and mixed.

II.   CRISIS: "A REFLECTION OF OUR RISK SOCIETY" (LAGADEC 1981) AND SOCIAL DEVELOPMENT

Why have there been increasing numbers of crises in recent years, particularly in the fields of the environment and health? An exhaustive list would be very long and certainly incomplete since there are serious crises that never transcend the boundaries of a sector or company. In virtually all cases of crisis, however, the media aspect is a major component. To suggest that the internationalization and detailed media coverage so dear to MacLuhan make an obvious contribution would not be out of line. Many facts that are at the root of crises today had undoubtedly already developed in the past but at a time when the media had not become omnipresent or acquired such speed of involvement, power, or ability to endow an event with dramatic, symbolic, and controversial importance. Certain events like Seveso (see Chapter 7) and Perrier (see Chapter 1) were neither disasters nor major risk situations, but the media gave them a scale that triggered the outbreak that was without doubt the root of the crisis.

The media are, of course, not the only ones to blame. Industrial society has increased technological risks with new processes, innumerable new products, new raw materials (which might be genetically modified), and economic pressures, which may have had a negative effect on safety levels.

At the same time, people have become far more aware of environmental damage (not only natural but social and human as well). This is also true of their focus on corporations, governments, and politicians. The psychological and ethical threshold of tolerance in certain risky situations has fallen significantly. Demands for managers and politicians to take responsibility (even to acknowledge accountability) have increased.

Overall, the thing that without doubt highlights the increasing number of crises is a profound change in the way our society understands certain events. Crises therefore offer a reflection of social development and observing them provides many points of analysis of our postindustrial society.

III.   CRISIS: THE SOUL OF THE CORPORATION REVEALED

The corporation has long been the barometer that measured the values industrial society prized most: performance, efficiency, growth, future. With economic recession and the ecology wave, the corporation lost much of its aura and experienced quite different and sometimes paradoxical developments. On the one hand, corporations felt the need to limit their negative impact on the environment. They therefore committed themselves to reducing chronic air and water pollution, to controlling waste and land pollution. The corporation wanted to become a good citizen. On the other hand, however, corporations were forced to ensure their survival—by keeping their shareholders' confidence—and had to keep an eye on the quality of their financial earnings. As a result, as markets became international, there was a wave of business closures, mergers, takeovers, restructuring, relocations, and layoffs. The consequences of this were substantial both externally, in the destabilization of regional economies, and internally, through weakened management and disinvestments. These trends were to be found in all industrial sectors and increased considerably the risks of a crisis in the case of a serious incident since they tended to foster a rapid loss of stability by the corporation.

Paradoxically, however, "it is often when corporations are confronted with what is for them a most unexpected event, to which they know not how to respond, that they reveal their true purpose in our society, sometimes being able to introduce courageous policies, free on this occasion of the artificialities of a fixed industrial image—a phenomenon which never fails to surprise journalists and employees" (Ogrizek 1993).

IV.   CRISIS, DECISION, AND COMMUNICATION

A crisis or a potential crisis demands that a decision be made and, almost simultaneously, that it be implemented and communicated. The risk, however, is high that things will get twisted and in particular that decision-making will become immediately subservient to the communication process intended to announce and explain the decision. This kind of communication may create major problems in an atmosphere of emergency, in the face of a complex situation full of uncertainty, with major economic stakes and strong media pressure. At times like this, managers may lose their decision- making ability and give way to the temptations of making an announcement just for the sake of effect. The message will be exaggeratedly reassuring, minimizing the risk in an attempt to justify the lack of any substantial decision. Or alternatively, some exceptional measure will be trumpeted to allow the company to cloak itself in an attitude of extreme precaution. In both cases, the decision-making itself has been supplanted by communication with a high risk of being inappropriate.

The problem of the necessary distinction between deciding and communicating is particularly hard since in an emergency the two stages are often intermingled. Speed and media exposure only add to the confusion. It is also true that in many crisis situations the essential decision to be made concerns precisely that communication process itself. For example, should the possibility of a risk about which almost nothing is now known and against which the measures to be taken might at best be only partial, be publicly revealed? Faced with such difficulties and such dilemmas, on what should an appropriate response be based?

In a crisis, the first requirement is to decide, then to communicate, and to be aware that a correct decision, to be understood and accepted, may require difficult and extended communication.

At a time of distress when a serious event calls for a decision, two questions should be asked in cold blood: First, what is the real risk and in particular what kind of risk is it? Second, what are the corporation's priority medium-term to long-term objectives? In other words, what sacrifices may be accepted and what is to be protected at all costs?

1

Product Risk and Crisis Communication

Mass-market consumer goods are just made to be victims of "popular crises" that reverberate loudly through the media. Their brand names carry powerful emotional and symbolic weight, they are highly visible and market-driven. In addition, these products are used frequently by a very large number of individuals, not to mention the fact that their quality and safety in use are monitored virtually constantly by both competitors and consumer organizations.

There are many situations that can cause a product crisis, including rumors, contamination (either accidental or criminal), accidents, and boycotts.

I. RUMORS

Rumors are "the oldest media in the world" (Kapferer 1987–1990) and still remain one of the main methods today for broadcasting negative views within a social group. Rumors always put official spokespersons (in this case industrial corporations and public authorities in charge, respectively, of managing and monitoring products available on the market) in an awkward position and sometimes even disrupt social order. They express the unspoken thoughts of a whole stratum of society, which circulates them without control, and—contrary to received thinking, which considers them to be the method of choice for disinformation—it is quite common for rumors to be well-founded.

Mass-market consumer goods convey a large amount of "official" information (promotional, technical, or regulatory), but they are also the subject of many underground comments shared every day, through word of mouth, by consumers influenced by all sorts of opinion. These may be personal, due to an unfortunate experience with a product; amusing or disturbing news related by friends who heard it from other friends; critical comparison with a competing product, presented by a salesperson as a confidence or advice; product-related risk, overtly denounced by a consumer-protection organization; various unbelievable facts related in the media; or a testimonial appeal as part of a consumer survey on a particular product. Mass-market consumer goods are in this way subject to a real "black market" (Kapferer 1987–1990) in information. Rumors based on this underground commentary are therefore, as a general rule, "the result of a process of collective discussion" (Shibutani 1996), which develops perniciously.

A. *The Mechanics of Rumor as a Form of Communication*

Rumors can start up and develop in various ways, which have been increasingly well catalogued by human science researchers.

1. Development.   In a crisis, it is not so much the source that needs to be identified (the unexpected appearance of a crisis almost always causes its victims to search in virtually paranoid fashion for a malicious instigator) as the way in which the rumor developed and took hold. That is really the first key component of diagnosis, which will then make it possible to contemplate anti-rumor measures best suited to the situation. A number of communication procedures can generate rumors about products:

a. Misappropriation.   Of either the product's original properties (e.g., rumors about "unofficial" secondary effects) or the common and popular product name (e.g., aerosols, which are called *bombs* in French, seem to carry connotations of the danger of explosion in the French collective unconscious).

b. Symbolism.   Between 1978 and 1982, there were rumors about worms in McDonald's hamburgers. These were considered by some sociologists to symbolize the rejection of food considered unhealthy by a certain stratum of the American population, who then proceeded to label it *junk food.*

c. Manipulation.   As suggested by worrying health information about food additives that circulated in the 1970s.

d. Extrapolation.   Rumor can arise from a real and anxiety-generating fact that implicates a particular product. The news then circulates and at the same time affects other products of the same type for no objective reason, but simply by analogy and assimilation.

e. Speculation. In the markets (e.g., rumors about commodities) or in medicine (e.g., rumors about the way AIDS is transmitted).

f. Explanation. Rumor opens people's eyes to details that had previously gone unnoticed and that are then seen for their true worth. It reveals hidden agendas. By deciphering the brand in the bar code, apparently commonplace and inoffensive consumer products, some people claim that they are marketed by the devil.

g. Resurgence of "floating myths," to adopt J.-N. Kapferer's (1987–1990) felicitous phrase. These are a particular kind of rumor. They often appear as "exemplary stories" in Véronique Campion-Vincent and Jean-Bruno Renard's (1992) terminology, or in other words as "mini–moral tales." They are thought to reflect our society's collective imagination, nourished since our earliest days by fantasies whose common roots are to be found in unconscious archetypes that form the basis of the culture in which they circulate. These "floating myths" are retold and updated to suit the tastes of the day. They can then be seen as real modern (urban) legends.

The themes of these "exemplary stories" are well-known to social anthropology researchers who have catalogued and studied them thoroughly. They produce "threats" that have circulated for centuries in the collective unconscious and that are experienced as dangers to the community's safety or to established social (moral) order. Examples include the fantasies of involuntary cannibalism and trade in human flesh, whether dead (ogre myth) or alive (white slave trade); the "foreign" threat affecting ethnic products and imports; the animal threat (getting revenge on humanity for its mistreatment); "invisible" threats (radioactivity, contaminating agents, or radiation waves from cell-phones, microwave ovens, and high-voltage power lines). Some of these threats may lie behind great fears.

2. Rumors Very Often Reflect a Latent Problem in Society. This is why they tend to develop against a background of demands by public opinion for security, of xenophobia, of racism, or of cultural (generation gap), religious, economic, political, or social tension.

The debate over the condition of women has fed rumors for years. Most of the risks to women's and family health become rumors that manifest themselves much more threateningly than the epidemiological reality (e.g., contraceptive pill, nylon panties, or hair dye). The blame attribution mechanism is often the driving force behind the rumor.

The debate over adolescents (and their teenage crisis) is also a permanent source of rumors that influence both their behavior and their products (e.g., jeans, Coke, or Pepsi).

Trade, ethnic, or religious tensions, for example, the secret purchase of domestic companies by "foreigners" and the satanic rumors, which became very frequent in the United States after 1978.

3.   Conditions for the Development of Rumors about Mass-Market Consumer Goods.   Conditions are best:

- *Prior to or during the launch:* The arrival of a new product upsets existing commercial balances.
- *At a time of technological innovation:* Rumor is one of the sociocultural representations of public resistance to change.
- *When a brand makes strong progress in the market:* One cannot help but suspect manipulation of competition.

This was the case, among other examples, for margarine, liquid detergent, phosphate-free detergent, fluoride in toothpaste, Teflon-coated pans, Pepsi Cola, alcohol-free beer, contact lenses, microwave ovens, video games, cellular phones, halogen lamps, PCs, Windows 95, and Airbus.

B.   Rumors and Crisis Communication

Rumors can have disastrous consequences for brands. At the very least, they affect a brand's image in the market, but in the long run they may also be responsible for a fall in sales or even lead to legal action by consumers who believe in good faith that they have suffered from their use.

"Let it be said straight away, there is no magic cure for controlling a rumor" (Kapferer 1987–1990). Each case has to be analyzed and a detailed diagnosis made. That said, several general rules of communication should be complied with to combat a rumor successfully. The first, which must be kept foremost in mind, is that rational discussion does not work, particularly when it is impossible to prove the truth, when the (technical) complexity of the problem raised by the rumor is hard to explain to the general public, or when the rumor is highly emotional. The second is that a credible source must be found if the struggle against rumor is to be successful, and that these days, most sources of information are not considered reliable by public opinion. In our modern society it is a fact that you can no longer trust (almost) anyone.

1.   It Might Be Tempting to Assume That the Rumor Will Die Naturally. Actually, when the victim is aware of the rumor and, even more so, when we are in the midst of overt crisis, the rumor has already acquired momentum of its own. It is not uncommon for the rumor's effects on sales of the affected product and/or the image of the corporation marketing it to be already significant. At this stage, waiting and hoping that the rumor will simply die by becoming unbelievable and therefore incapable of transmission, is illusory. In addition, a crisis rumor is often already in the media, which nourish it, exaggerate it, add to it and, most seriously, give it the gloss of news.

2. *It Might Be Tempting to Treat Rumor with Irony.*   Information broadcast in ironical tones aimed at showing that the statements peddled are grotesque may be taken at face value! Beware, irony is the mother of rumor.

3. *The Conditions in Which a Rumor Spreads Reveal the Tactics to Be Deployed against It.*   "The audience for a rumor includes those who feel themselves affected by the consequences of this event" (Kapferer 1987–1990). As long as there are willing ears and tongues (involved listeners) free to hear and pass on the contained message, the rumor will continue to spread.

a. *Saturating all the listeners still available*   is therefore, in theory and based on this evidence, the best way to treat a rumor. If all those who are likely to hear and convey the rumor already know it, what is the attraction of passing it on to someone else who is already "in the know"? There is virtually no more "secondary personal benefit" [1] of being the source of the revelation. "Once a rumor is called a rumor by the public, it runs out of steam" (Kapferer 1987–1990).

A simple denial is not sufficient to saturate all the listeners involved and is therefore, as a general rule, ineffective. Most of the time a denial is very badly received by the media and when it is published, it is published *only once* and often late. As a result, it almost always passes unnoticed—it is no more than a drop in the ocean of rumor. It is not credible since it has been issued by a source that is the victim of the rumor. In addition, when the denial is clumsy in addressing the subject of the rumor, it will then remain negatively associated in people's minds with the rumor event. *The rumor to which one has fallen victim must never be repeated.* It is also important to realize that "one can be negatively influenced by a denial even if people believe it" (Kapferer 1987–1990). The following communication techniques should be implemented to thwart these perverse effects and make action against rumors more effective.

b. *Rumor disassociation and reassociation.*   These are two crisis communication techniques that may improve quality control of the rumor:

Disassociation aims to break the unequivocal and direct analogy between product X and the specific negative information conveyed by the rumor. In this case, the rumor is generalized to include other products of the same kind.

Reassociation consists in offsetting the negative factors with positive factors or even in injecting into the rumor features that are morally unacceptable to the dominant culture. If the rumor is socially or culturally unacceptable, it will be rejected and its authors with it. That is how in Orleans, France, the rumor about young girls disappearing in clothing stores in this small provincial French city ended: the story appeared to become anti-Semitic, which was then considered intolerable by intellectuals, organizations, politicians, and the media (Morin 1976).

4. *If There Is a Rumor, It Is Essential to Introduce a System That Makes It Possible to Track It (by Mapping):* To assess in real time how it is being broadcast both in sociological and geographical terms as well as to note changes in themes (which may open other routes for it to spread).

5. *Resistance to Treatment.* Managers of corporations who fall victim to a rumor generally do not wish to give broad publicity to stories circulating about one of their products: the less known the better. The fact of the matter is that by not telling the largest possible number of relevant listeners about the rumor they are virtually guaranteeing that it will be sustained.

6. *Products and Institutions.* The main principles of product rumor management are valid also for managing rumors about people and institutions. Major industrial groups sign their names on product ranges: there is no boundary between the product name and the company's name. Any rumor that affects the product will therefore also tarnish the corporation, and vice versa. Rumors just love language's vessels of communication.

II.   PRODUCT CONTAMINATION

Product contamination is much more frequent than we think. In the last seven years, for example, more than a thousand products have been contaminated and there are estimated to have been nearly three hundred cases of extortion.

A.   Accidental Contamination

Such cases may have natural or industrial causes. By virtue of its very products, the food industry is without question the highest-risk industrial sector. The list is long.

The crisis that offers the best lessons, however, is without doubt the Perrier crisis. It contains all the basic requirements of a product crisis caused by accidental industrial contamination.

The Perrier Crisis: A Case Study

The Initial Facts

Discovery of Contamination and Withdrawal from Sale.

February 7, 1990:   The company is informed of the discovery of benzene traces in Perrier bottles by an analytical laboratory in North Carolina.

February 9, 1990:   The company decides to withdraw Perrier bottles from sale in the United States. Analysis confirms the presence of benzene traces in Perrier bottles at the Vergèze production site. Delays in replacing a filter in the carbon dioxide gas channel are assumed responsible.

February 11, 1990:   Benzene traces are revealed in Perrier bottles in Europe.

February 14, 1990:   The decision to withdraw 160 million bottles of Perrier around the world is announced by chairman Gustave Leven at a press conference.

New Production and Product Relaunch.

March 7, 1990:   New production with changed label. Product available in both France and Europe.

April 1990:   Product available in the United States and Japan. "New Perrier" production boycotted in the United Kingdom by a retail chain.

June 1990:   A sparkling mineral water closely resembling Perrier is marketed in Britain.

September/October 1990:   Perrier's general and operating management is thoroughly restructured under pressure from major shareholders. Dingell Committee (U.S. Congress) inquiry into the conditions for producing mineral water in Europe.

November 1990:   New labels are stuck on competing brands indicating that the water has natural gas added.

1992:   Nestlé mounts a takeover bid for Perrier. Planned restructuring of company and Vergèze production operations.

The Ten Lessons of the Perrier Crisis

<u>*Lesson 1:*</u>   *Globalization of production (global sourcing) tends to assist international crises.*   The Perrier crisis is virtually a caricature of a crisis caused

by global sourcing: the existence of a single source of supply for a unique raw material and a single production site for the finished product (regulations require mineral waters to be bottled where they are drawn).

Lesson 2:   *A company may be forced to withdraw a product from the market to comply with its market positioning.*   A qualitative health and/or ecological claim will permanently overexpose a product's brand image and the credibility of the company that sells it.

Everyone in France knew the famous advertising formula *Perrier, c'est fou!* (Perrier is crazy!) but withdrawing 160 million bottles was *really* crazy! Many journalists did not hesitate to stress the point. That was not the main reason for the recall, however, as some people may naively have believed ("a fantastic advertising coup"). The product's positioning in the North American market, summarized in the definitive slogan "It's perfect," already contained a popular verdict, which brooked no appeal. The advertising claimed that Perrier water was pure and the presence of benzene traces, even minute ones carrying no danger to consumers' health, was incompatible with this basic claim. Withdrawing 60 million bottles from the North American market was simply a demonstration of marketing consistency and corporate honesty, whatever the cost. The recall was the only possible decision, the only culturally appropriate one. Gustave Leven revealed this corporate decision at a press conference on February 14, 1990.

Was that a good enough reason to justify the decision, however, and to convince the general public that the operation was well founded? How would he explain to the skeptics that Perrier had taken this unprecedented decision to withdraw its product from the worldwide market at great cost if there was actually no health risk for consumers and no health authority had prohibited its sale? It was essential to be very clear on this point. Otherwise, the notion—and the rumor—could have developed, unconsciously, that the company was in fact hiding something more serious from both the authorities and the public. This was all the more true since this event took place against a very particular background: "A company which has always cultivated secrets, like water diviners . . ."

Lesson 3:   *Quality control only unearths what it is looking for and new analysis technology makes it possible to discover traces of almost anything in almost everything.*   The discovery of benzene traces in Perrier was made by an external laboratory. It has become a classic case. External monitoring of product quality is carried out not only by official organizations, but also by competitors and consumer associations' laboratories. New analysis technology has made it possible in only a few years to progress from identifying parts per million to revealing parts per billion without it being possible to ascribe any real toxicological risk to consumers from the presence of these minute traces! It is easy to understand the communication difficulties in such a situation: there is something there, but it has no known significance. What should be done? In addition, it has been well demonstrated that small figures never reassure people: conceptualizing statistical risk is not an easy subject for the media. From now on, precautionary measures will dominate institutional behavior or, in other words, "If in doubt, cut it out!" The voluntary recall of products from the market at the slightest doubt has become the current industrial expression of this rule. As a result, we are now in a world where mass-market consumer products have never been safer from a health standpoint and yet have never been regarded with as much suspicion.

Lesson 4: *The gap between popular terminology and scientific terminology for designating a product's properties may be the source of some confusion in public opinion and may force the authorities to refocus regulations.* In the middle of the crisis, a British newspaper ran the headline: "Perrier Water Is Not Drinking Water." It's true! By regulatory definitions, mineral waters are not drinking water. Strictly speaking, the standards establishing whether water is drinking water or not stipulate concentrations of minerals that for the most part are actually well below levels found in mineral waters. That does not mean, of course, that mineral waters are not safe to drink. It is simply a matter of definitions, which make it possible to approve or reject water as fitting in the category of mineral drinks.

Lesson 5: *A product crisis always tends to become general and ends up, by analogy, tarnishing other products in the same industrial sector.* In the months that followed the announcement that Perrier was contaminated with benzene for instance, the media gave voice to doubts—based on summer drought and concerns about the quality of the groundwater in France—about the abnormal presence of nitrates, organochlorine compounds, saprophytes, and pathogens, as well as traces of insecticides, fungicides, and pesticides, not only in other mineral waters (both sparkling and still), but also in other drinks such as soft drinks and wine.

Lesson 6: *To save essential and long-term attributes, it is important to be able to sacrifice information that will worsen the crisis in the short term.* Crisis communication is a delicate exercise in controlled information transparency. Many works written for managers recommend telling "the truth, the whole truth, and nothing but the truth." This is a rather simplistic view. Production secrets, contracts with confidential or even suspensive clauses, medical data in the event of an accident, or financial data during the acquisition of shares in a takeover bid are all situations that sometimes demand silence, or at least the traditional "No comment" of Anglo-American institutions. Controlled transparency can be summarized in the concise formula: "Everything you say must be true."

In order to explain the operating incident that led to the product being contaminated with benzene and, in doing so, to show that the spring water, which some incorrectly claimed to be contaminated, was clean, Perrier had to reveal publicly, in detail and for the first time, that the spring water and carbon dioxide gas were in fact pumped separately for several miles, transported in different pipes to the factory and finally mixed just before bottling. Then and only then did it became clear that the incident, which involved the failure to replace a filter in the carbon dioxide gas system, could not have affected the water quality in any way. Revealing the real industrial production conditions in this way had the enormous advantage of removing any doubts about the quality of the spring water, showing that the technical problem behind the contamination could be resolved easily and, in sum, ensuring that the product would survive. On the other hand, this truth had the enormous disadvantage of revealing that Perrier had for a long time not been "naturally sparkling mineral water." The label that stated this on every bottle was therefore inaccurate in that the sparkling water was not extracted intact from the ground at Vergèze but was actually reconstituted at the plant to comply with its original natural composition. The lesser of two evils has to be chosen. Not telling the truth amounted to exposing the Perrier source to all the rumors of pollution and as a result running the risk of condemning the product to death. Telling the truth amounted to saving the essential part, the source, but being subject (particularly in the United States and the United Kingdom) to the media's opprobrium for this culture of hiding information as well as serious technical and regulatory difficulties. That is why Perrier now carries a white label on the neck of the bottle stating, "Fortified with gas from the spring," and so does Badoit! ("re-aerated with its own gas").

   Lesson 7:   *An international crisis is first and foremost a crisis of cross-cultural communication.*   The reactions of consumers, the press, and the authorities to the announcement of Perrier's contamination with benzene traces varied by both country and culture.

   In France, Perrier was part of the social and cultural heritage, in the same way as Dior and Chanel no. 5. When the recall was announced, consumers literally rushed to points of sale to buy Perrier. Out of fear of not having any? This is a very French sociological reaction, which has been seen in several food scares, such as the sugar speculation in 1974. Then, over subsequent weeks, with the assistance of a little snobbishness, it became trendy among the in-crowd to demand, jokingly, a "real Perrier," with benzene understood. People continued to do this even when the new production was available. In this black market atmosphere, some bars, hotels, and restaurants did not return their stock, preferring to run down the precious drink complicitly with the consumer. It was particularly easy and carried no legal risk since, it should be recalled, "Perrier with benzene" was never banned from sale by the health authorities given the absence of any danger to consumer health. For an individual to be exposed to even the tiniest risk, he or she would had to have drunk an Olympic swimming pool of Perrier each day since the brand had been created! The vague feeling that this was an attack by the Americans who wanted to put down French products or a good example of protectionism was not divorced from incredulity that there might be a real problem of accidental contamination.

In the United States, Perrier capitalized on sociocultural difference in a Coca Cola world. In this market, withdrawing a product, however much of a status symbol it might be, always exposes it to rapid substitution in consumer behavior, particularly when the core target consumers are a fickle social group easily swayed by fashion (such as New York yuppies) and when the competition has enormous resources for winning back market share. The core strategy, therefore, was to occupy space at points of sale and to ensure that the brand was visible. Local communication with consumers was organized quickly. This consisted in creating a real ghost market in anticipation of the launch of the new product by continuing to rent space on shelves at the main points of sale and filling them constantly with empty packaging and/or little posters announcing day after day the schedule for the return of Perrier.

In Japan, mineral water was an exotic drink from France, a luxury product in the same way as cognac or champagne. What counted under these conditions was reassurance that the consumer was consuming the original brand. Still today, some Japanese have cases of mineral water delivered by mail order, just as in Europe people have cases of wine delivered directly from the vineyard. A new label identifying original production was the best reassurance.

Under similar circumstances, it is essential to assess public opinion, particularly consumers' views on the decision to withdraw the product, to test the effectiveness of advertising messages and other actions, and finally to anticipate consumer behavior when the product is relaunched. Regular opinion surveys in key markets are essential guides to acting in the most appropriate manner in a crisis (headlines are only the visible part of the opinion iceberg and may not reflect what people really think about the issue at all). For the company they represent a way of communicating. One of the major problems of a product withdrawal is management of the post-recall period. Either the product is not relaunched (that would have been the case if the source had been polluted) or it is relaunched (that was the case since the gas contamination was a technical problem that was easy to resolve). In the first case, the risk is to the corporate image and not to the product. In the second case, applicable to Perrier, the risk is to the brand and the product's survival on the market. Meeting this challenge of necessity calls for a period of winning back market share. It is good then to be able to say loud and long, and to prove, that consumers support the corporation and have confidence in the brand and the product! Opinion surveys carried out by Burson-Marsteller in France, Great Britain, the United States, and Canada showed that "most consumers, nine out of ten drinkers of the mineral water, had been kept fully informed of the incident. A large majority of Perrier consumers had understood that the product represented no danger to their health and on the whole, the public felt that Perrier had acted in an exemplary manner. A very large majority of Perrier drinkers firmly intended to drink Perrier again as soon as it was available."

Lesson 8: _A serious crisis affecting a major product is the start of a long series of crises for a company (see Figure 1)._   In the short term, a production crisis leads, of necessity, to a product crisis, which de facto tarnishes the brand marketing image.

In the medium term, this almost always leads to a regulatory crisis with new controls and a redefinition of operating standards; a management crisis with the ejection of the main managers responsible and reorganization of sales strategies; and a shareholder crisis with a takeover (either hostile or friendly) and redistribution of the interests at stake.

In the longer term, the internal impact of all these painful events weakens the company and brings its technical and cultural habits into question. It is then forced to face up to a very profound corporate identity crisis

Figure 1. Vicious circle of product crises.

which leads typically to wide-ranging industrial restructuring and/or the successive emergence of major labor crises. A product also remains tarnished forever by a major crisis. Every time something happens to it, there is instant media visibility. It also becomes a target for all the media vultures who are trying to find a method or communication platform to establish themselves quickly. In Belgium in 1996, for example, summer Perrier advertising was called sexist by a women's movement. This story immediately made the headlines and forced the posters to be withdrawn. Communication consultants who had never worked on the case suggested that they were part of this extraordinary media adventure to lend credibility to their expertise in crisis management.

Lesson 9: *Major crises sear themselves into collective industrial memories and change professional behavior.* The Perrier crisis is now a part of the industrial collective unconscious. When a product is accidentally contaminated, company managers immediately refer to the Perrier case and consider the immediate recall of their product from the market. In fact, the Perrier case has very often been presented as a success story and several commentators have even speculated about the publicity motivations behind the recall. Each year many products that might not have been withdrawn from sale fall victim to the Perrier syndrome and are withdrawn.

Lesson 10: *A crisis is an open system.* A crisis can start up again at any time—either at Perrier or by destabilizing another mineral water company. Water is a vital product, one that is highly symbolic of well-being and health in our civilization. There are more than a thousand mineral springs in France and no summer ever goes by without worries about drought, reserves of drinking water, and pollution of groundwater. Our collective imagination retains many rumors just asking to reemerge, together with old and everlasting ecological debates whose only purpose seems to be to occupy the summer headlines, such as radioactivity in the water of certain drinks, contamination of running water with heavy metals, or germ pollution of tap water.

B. Criminal Contamination

This remains a frequent and serious threat, particularly in Great Britain, Ireland, Germany, Italy, the United States, and Japan. It is a permanent sword of Damocles over the heads of the food, cosmetics, and pharmaceuticals industries.

1. Methods of Contamination. Criminal contamination usually attacks mass-market consumer products that have high emotional and symbolic potential. It is therefore no accident that chocolate and jars of baby food tend to be favorite targets. The consumer is virtually no more than an innocent bystander whose death will be perceived as intolerable by public opinion. For this reason, institutional catering is also a potential target.

All OTC medicines (over the counter, i.e., sold without a doctor's prescription and freely available in pharmacies in Britain and the United States), particularly those intended for children, are naturally high-risk products. The contamination of Johnson & Johnson's Tylenol in 1982 has also become a case study.

Cosmetics are generally subject to a specific symbolic threat: blackmail using poison or acid—the horror of disfiguring spawned by the desire to be beautiful. This type of atavistic and historical fantasy will naturally be reactivated and enhanced by some of the mass-market press whose specialty it has become.

Large corporate brands are the first to be targeted, for two main reasons: (1) their brand name is generic—it encompasses a series of different products, increasing the immediacy of the threat in the consumer's mind; (2) they belong to major industrial groups; and in the blackmailer's mind, these firms have the resources to pay a large sum of money quickly.

a. Criminal contamination often appears in the form of blackmail, either linked to an extortion demand for money or in relation to extremist moral or political issues. It should be borne in mind that to move from a threat to the act itself is exceptional, but in the midst of a crisis it is very hard to assess the risk of this happening. There are, however, other motivations and, under these circumstances, it is not unusual for the crime already to have been committed. Such motives include revenge, perversion, and collective suicide crimes (such as by sects).

b. One type of criminal contamination on the rise is sabotage by a professional at the source, i.e., on the production site or at a storage warehouse. This usually happens when the company is undergoing restructuring with the threat of final plant closure. The source of such a drama might also be a single, individual layoff seen as abusive by an emotionally unbalanced employee.

c. Criminal contamination generally uses dangerous substances or materials that are easy to buy or—more rarely—products used in the trade. The most frequently used contaminants in Europe are cyanide, rat poison, and razor blades.

d. Criminal contamination is often preannounced, particularly when it is a matter of blackmail. The criminal will make an advance demonstration of his or her capability to contaminate a product, telling the company's managers, or more infrequently the police, in what exact place (for example, a supermarket) they will find a sample of the contaminated product, containing either a dangerous material or an inoffensive substance (such as methylene blue). This is the classic so-called "stated intent to kill" strategy.

e. There are real epidemics of criminal contamination. In March 1989 in Great Britain, several hundred jars of baby food were sabotaged with razor blades, glass shards, pins, and caustic soda. In May of the same year in Belgium and France, another brand of baby food was found to contain needles and thumbtacks. In 1984, chocolate fell victim to such an epidemic in France and Great Britain. One must not underestimate the power of copycat incidents. In June 1993, in the United States, Diet Pepsi experienced over thirty-five (false) claims of contamination in twenty states within forty-eight hours.

2. Criminal Contamination and Crisis Communication. Managing such a situation means meeting two operating targets: *consumer safety* and *corporate ethics.*

There are several essential rules:

- Never give in to blackmail. (Unfortunately, there are no statistics available to reflect the value of such advice.)
- Corporate communication must be managed in very close collaboration with the police authorities in charge of the inquiry.
- It is recommended that the product be withdrawn from the market, but this will not solve everything! Criminal contamination could actually affect a number of products at any one time.

There are enormous difficulties in managing such a crisis: It is still easy to withdraw a product targeted by criminal contamination at the production stage (by stopping production lines) and the distribution stage (by freezing stocks and emptying store shelves) from sale. The real problem—and it is a big one since there is the potential risk of panic—is how to recall, effectively and quickly, products that have already been bought and are in the home. Consumers may use them at any moment and some of them may die! The only solution in practice is therefore to warn consumers directly through the mass media in order to avoid any further possible deaths. Communicating in such a way obviously brings exposure to the risk of journalistic license being used in reproducing the warning message, of deviation both in how the message is formulated and how it is perceived, and quite naturally of some anxiety building in consumers' minds.

Morally, however, it is almost always the only approach possible. The 1994 Josacine case is an example of this.

The Josacine Crisis: A Case Study

When analysis confirmed the presence of cyanide in the bottle of antibiotics that had killed Emilie, a nine-year-old girl, nobody was able to say whether it was an isolated criminal act involving a single bottle (how otherwise could the murder of a good child in a family with no previous history be explained?) or the beginning of a much more wide-ranging case of criminal contamination, which might affect the safety of several bottles of the same medicine. It was totally impossible to choose between these two scenarios and there were complicating circumstances such as the use of a substance that is always fatal a few minutes after absorption; a ban on specifying the nature of the poison to the public, straightaway and clearly, so as not to disturb the investigation by revealing too soon to the assassin that the investigators had identified the weapon; and a race against the clock that afternoon with hundreds of thousands of spoonfuls of this syrup already prescribed in France for that very evening. It was clearly a moral emergency: the pharmaceutical company had to inform without delay the hundreds of thousands of parents in possession of this syrup so that they could be stopped from giving it to their children before bedtime. Only the media power of the 8:00 P.M. national television and radio news programs could stop a fatal move in time, since they reached directly into virtually all French homes. Neither a dispatch from Agence France Presse nor an unequivocal note from the pharmacists or the prescribing doctors would have had a high probability of suspending the latent risk of another child's death. The former is reproduced secondarily and therefore later and with no guarantee of success. The latter would have taken more than two days, assuming that these professional intermediaries had lists of patients to whom they had prescribed the medicine, including names, addresses, and telephone numbers, which was not the case in reality. The absolute priority therefore was not to inform health care professionals first, but to avoid a further family tragedy by openly revealing the risk to parents. The question to put to the critics of this communications operation is actually very simple: How much time or how many innocent deaths would they have required in order to justify mass public dissemination of the information? It is always easy to diagnose an isolated fatal incident after a suspect has been arrested.

The media's announcement of the risk of death generated more than seven thousand calls from parents and professionals in the first few hours.

The callers often expressed intense emotion, but the thanks of hundreds of parents who had been preparing to administer the syrup were just as heartfelt. In opinion surveys among doctors, pharmacists, and a representative sample of the general population, more than 80 percent of the respondents understood, respected, and were even grateful for the pharmaceutical company's decision. This lesson in industrial ethics also challenged health care authorities at the time. They have as a result been persuaded to consider a system of emergency information for health care professionals under similar circumstances.

III. ACCIDENTS

Product-induced accidents can in turn lead to situations of complicated sociodrama (ranging from a simple news item to a full-fledged disaster) or can be the source of major public fears reflecting real collective crises of confidence.

A. *Classifying Product Accidents*

Examples are well-documented, each raising specific challenges that call for appropriate measures.

1. *Accidents Involving the Product's Intrinsic Qualities*

a. Defective products.   Defects may result from a production fault or from contamination, among other causes.

- In this case, the real jeopardy from the communication standpoint is that *the affected brand might be tarnished.*
- *It is essential to withdraw the product from sale.* Depending on information gathered by product defect tracking systems, management must decide between total recall of the product from the market or only a partial batch recall. A partial recall may take the form of recall and exchange (replacement of the defective product with another fault-free product) or recall and check, which makes it possible either to reassure the consumer or to repair or exchange a defective product.

If the company does not undertake the recall voluntarily, the authorities are likely to impose an order banning the product's sale or, at least, suspending its marketing. If the defective product were left on the market with the approval of the authorities pending technical confirmation of the real risk to the user, this might trigger a passive boycott (out of suspicion or fear) or even the development of an active boycott initiated by a consumer protection organization. In the long run, the risk of legal action against the manufacturer must not be ruled out.

b. Defects in the industrial process. The real danger here from the communication standpoint is that the whole industrial sector's image might be tarnished. In the case of a domestic pet food brand, health accidents potentially due to sterilization problems could cast doubt on all brands using the same production process.

- *Voluntary recall of the directly incriminated brand is essential* and calls for the same process of providing information as in the case of a defective product.
- *General communication by the industry about good production practices and product quality control is essential.* The secondary risk in such a situation is that new and more restrictive regulations, which are generally more costly for the industry, will be introduced. Legal action against the manufacturer is not uncommon.

2. Accidents Involving the Conditions of Product Use

a. Misuse of the product. Failure to comply with instructions can lead to serious accidents. The instructions and warnings found in leaflets and on packaging are key factors in the direct communication of safety information to the user. They must therefore be drafted very clearly (free of technical jargon) and presented in perfectly readable print. Pictures can be used to illustrate the kind of danger involved such as for poisonous or flammable products. Regulations are becoming increasingly strict in this regard and consumer organizations are highly vigilant about the enforcement of rules. Domestic accidents are actually a permanent threat in today's society. The statistics speak volumes. They show clearly the need for campaigns to inform and educate the population on safe behavior in the home such as systematically storing medicines and household articles out of the reach of children.

When there are repeated accidents with a particular type of product, the product will probably be implicated itself (and not just its use by incompetent, negligent, or careless users!). Similar competing products and their manufacturers will then often be in the line of fire. A crisis very often develops following the publication of a report by a consumer protection organization comparing products.

New labeling or new packaging is essential. The authorities will be sorely tempted to make regulatory demands that labeling and packaging be changed or even that certain packaging be discontinued if it is not conducive to good use. If the accident receives strong media coverage (if it involves a child, for example), legal action should be expected or even organized action calling for testimonials and active boycotts.

b. Deviant product use by consumers. Some drug addicts seek readily available everyday products for the "high" they can get. The best-known example is glue. There are endless rumors about the side effects of some products.

In these cases, the product is taken hostage by the philosophical, social, and political debate that overtakes it. Deviant product use rapidly becomes an epiphenomenon and the product crisis is suddenly widespread. This is how a particular product or a category of products may become genuine symbols of the crisis in our Western society, as is the case with Valium and tranquilizers.

If the frequency of deviant product use becomes a matter of concern in health terms, technical measures (e.g., reformulation along with a search for repellent effects) aimed at discouraging potential addicts (or potential suicides) are essential. The commercial risk is that the authorities will introduce new regulations aimed at tightening conditions of sale for the affected product.

3. Accidents Involving a Manufacturer's or a Professional's Behavior

a. Professional fault, error or negligence in choosing or applying products: If repeated, this kind of accident can end up altering the image of a whole industry for good. Accidents caused by anesthetic products, for instance, give rise to news items that always get too much coverage and very emotionally reawaken the fear of operations in the collective imagination. Other products are just as regularly implicated when it comes to questionable professional application, including pesticides and fertilizers. The accusations of misuse made by ecologists never fail to tarnish the image of farmers in the public mind.

The risk is that a scapegoat syndrome will develop, both for the product—chlorine is a good example—and for the person who chooses it. For example, in certain cultures an individual may be presumed guilty or at least suspect, simply because his or her skin is black. Professional fault, errors, and negligence almost automatically result in legal action initiated by the complaints of the victims or their families.

b. Unethical marketing on the part of manufacturers. The product is dangerous and the manufacturer knows it, but continues to market it. A tragic example is the untreated blood contaminated with HIV that was given to hemophiliacs.

In the event of unethical behavior by one or several managers, they must be laid off for gross misconduct and legal action taken by the industrial corporation's new management. These decisions should be given substantial media coverage and there must be candid internal communication on the matter. For a corporation the risk is that for many months or even years it will be the focus of a painful legal and media scandal.

B. Mechanics of the Product Accident Crisis

Any Product-Related Accident Leads to a Search for the Responsible Party. This is simply one of the cornerstones of crisis dynamics.

   1. The public tends to be confused over the difference between responsibility and guilt,   particularly since under law an industrial corporation is often held responsible for all the secondary effects of its products, including risks not yet identified or considered.
   The famous formula "responsible but not guilty," which was used in France by politicians in the contaminated blood scandal, and the resulting tarnishing of their personal image in the eyes of the French public shows how difficult it is to distinguish between these two concepts.

   2. It is not always easy to work out who is responsible.   This is particularly true for certain types of product that are chronically in crisis:
   Airplanes: Air crashes are the perfect example of mixed questions. Was it individual pilot error, a product design fault (cockpit electronics or ergonomics), negligent maintenance, external circumstances (a bomb or the weather), inadequate further pilot training, corporate or regulatory responsibility (two pilots rather than three with a navigator on board)?
   Cigarettes: The prevalent debate and the type of crises to which it has led are particularly instructive. If smoking is medically acknowledged to be dangerous for smokers (causing lung cancer and cardiovascular disease), then who is responsible: the individual (smokers are warned of the risks), society (passive smoking), or organizations (manufacturers or the authorities who approve the sale of cigarettes)?

C. A Crisis Is Particularly Acute If the Public Perceives a Major Risk

Perception of the size of the risk is based on two important parameters: closeness and the feeling of not being able to control the situation.

<u>The idea of closeness</u> emerges suddenly at the time of the accident. When news breaks of a problem with a product in current use, many people will realize that they or their loved ones have often used it. Dramatic and re-

peated media coverage of the event will only increase this impression of the danger being close.

The feeling of loss of control also substantially increases the perception of risk and encourages the onset of crisis. A large part of the population accepts the risk of road travel, whereas an airplane accident immediately arouses violent media emotions. Car drivers all have the illusion that they will be able to keep control of their vehicle, even in unexpectedly difficult situations. Passengers in an airplane, on the other hand, know that they will have no chance of influencing the outcome of the event.

In many potential crisis situations, communication must aim in particular to limit the possible unwarranted or exaggerated perception of closeness or loss of control. In some cases, the idea of voluntary or semivoluntary risk-taking may arise.

D. A Golden Rule

It is essential to understand that product crises are not handled by the product manager but must include the executive in charge of marketing and the CEO. It is the whole corporation that is being targeted and questioned through the product. Anything that can affect a major brand has to be managed overall by top management. There is enormous financial risk since a major brand is one of the most important measures of the corporation's economic value. [2]

Crises experienced by brands such as Philip Morris (cigarette filter contamination), Intel Pentium (computation error), Omo (detergent powder causing clothes to deteriorate in the wash), and Perrier (benzene traces) are there as spectacular reminders.

IV.   BOYCOTTS

A boycott call is a very specific kind of product crisis: it is often caused by moral, religious, political, or ecological questions.

A.   A Boycott Is Rarely an Effective Measure

Each year there are about two hundred boycott calls worldwide, but most of them fail to break out of the restricted circle of ghostly militant organizations that have few resources to make their voices heard. After a media announcement and one or two articles in underground newspapers—both specialized and ephemeral—the boycott generally dies even before it is born in terms of average consumer behavior. Boycotts still, however, cause fear because some, sustained by powerful organizations such as Greenpeace or certain Anglo-American church groups that operate like real multinationals with substantial financial and logistical resources, have had the benefit of large-scale media coverage.

B. Assessment of the Real Risk Presented by a Boycott

To have any chance of success, a boycott has to comply with several fundamental strategic and operational rules. Assessing the real risk of a boycott means reviewing the following criteria:

- *Closeness.* A company's product, brand, service, or chain that is highly visible in the market and very close to consumers' everyday lives will be very vulnerable.
- *Substitution.* If the product or service offered is neither specific nor exclusive it can easily be replaced by another of similar kind or the same quality. The concept of substitution makes it easier to act.
- *Passivity and proactivity.* A boycott may be passive (I decide not to go ahead and buy the product because the reason for the boycott dawns on me at the moment of purchase) or proactive (I have already decided from the start that I will not buy this product or that I will not use this service out of principle; in this case the customer type is often a militant consumer).

C. Reasons

1. Ethical Reasons. The reasons behind many boycott calls are religious, philosophical, ecological, and/or humanitarian considerations.

If one looks at new social anthropological trends, it is clear that there is currently tactical and operational convergence of boycott calls for human rights reasons and for natural environment reasons.

Ethical (and safety) reasons increasingly lead governments and international organizations to take active official boycott measures in regulatory or legislative form (including embargoes, quotas, bans, withdrawal from the market, and refusal of approval). In fact, these are very often excuses for protectionism.

Boycotts are often transposed. In the 1970s, Nestlé milk powder was boycotted in the United States because the company marketed the product in Third World countries. This is the ultimate historical reference case for this kind of boycott. It has since served as a lesson, for example, for boycotts in the United States against the products of international firms operating in South Africa during the apartheid years.

2. Reasons of Individual and Collective Safety. These are further reasons for boycotts that express doubts about the safety of a product or service.

When safety reasons do not give rise to official boycott measures (such as the banning or suspension of sale), they generally lead to a passive boycott by consumers (out of fear) and calls for active boycotts from organizations. Mad cow disease is a good example. In 1996, consumption of beef in European countries dropped by an average of 11 percent.

D. Support

Few organizations are capable of managing a large-scale boycott and making it effective. Greenpeace succeeded in achieving this in Germany (in the Brent Spar case), but only for a few weeks.

1. *Political and Institutional Back-Up Is Essential If a Boycott Is to Succeed over the Longer Term.*   That is why professional boycotters will try very quickly to initiate a political and governmental process by mobilizing elected representatives sympathetic to their cause, in the hopes of obtaining an official boycott (in the form of a resolution or new regulation).

2. *Media Support Is Essential to Keep a Boycott Alive.*   Proactive, high-profile, and symbolic spokespersons are needed as well as a good emotional story based on good conscience and partisan economic interests.

E. The Schedule

A call for a boycott on ethical grounds has to be made at the right moment. The anniversary, for example, of the liberation or death of a symbolic personality, or an official visit by such a person. Summer is a good time in the media but a very bad time for mobilizing consumers (unless the aim is to boycott sun cream products or trips to a foreign country with an unacceptable political regime).

F. A Boycott Often Includes Specific Actions

These actions are aimed at drawing attention, reawakening awareness, harassing the targeted institution, or destabilizing its commercial, financial, and political allies. Examples include demonstrations and media guerrilla tactics such as the occupation of a company's premises, physical destruction of company properties, external and internal leaflets, badgering and disturbing employees by telephone and fax (the harassment technique), petitions signed by employees then broadcast by the media, open letters to newspapers in the form of advertising inserts, hijacking of advertising slogans, and letter bombs.

G. What to Do When Faced with a Boycott Call

1. *Never Overreact.*   A boycott *call* is not a boycott. It will take time to move consumers on to action beyond the noisy mobilization of a hard core

of activists. Time is always on the side of those faced with a boycott.

When the call is made, and only if it has high media coverage, the company should once and for all clearly and publicly state its position on the matter to the journalists, its main political and commercial partners, and its staff. Having stated its position, the company must never go back on it.

2.   Remember the Main Basic Principles of Crisis Communication When Faced with a Boycott

a.   The ones who have communication problems are those who make the boycott call, not those who suffer the boycott! The challenge for the boycotters is actually to make the wider public aware of the boycott and the reasons behind it, and above all to keep it alive long enough for it to have an effect. It is known that it takes an average of five years of continuous and sustained communication to have a long-term effect on the marketing of a brand.

b.   If the boycotted company tries to communicate too much, it will make the boycott more visible in the eyes of the public and as a result, in wishing clumsily to defend itself, will help the boycotters communicate their case! When faced with a boycott, therefore, it is necessary to adopt the lowest possible profile in external communications.

c.   On the other hand, internal communication is a top priority. It should be open, strong and personalized (the company chairman should vouch for it personally). It should state clearly to staff and unions that the boycott is unjust and inform them of the company's position on the issues raised by the boycotters. It is essential that direct operating information be given (as well as guidelines for behavior) to managers of subsidiaries at risk so that they may pass it on to managers of the various businesses in the field and in doing so avoid as much as possible the major risk of deviation following unfortunate local initiatives with the public, customers, and media.

d.   Priority must also be given to communicating with major shareholders, suppliers, and above all customers! The latter may actually become specific targets since the primary target can be weakened by boycotting its customers directly.

e.   It is essential to keep national and local governmental organizations informed to try and avoid ill-timed statements or measures through simple ignorance of the issues or, worse, through political opportunism.

f.   At sensitive times, both the product and the corporation should keep a low profile. Priorities:

- Stop all advertising campaigns in countries where there is a boycott.
- Reduce the visibility of signs and logos.
- Cancel certain promotional activities.
- Delay any new launches within the boycotted product range.

g. Surveys should be carried out regularly among the general public and at-risk consumers to measure the degree of awareness of the boycott and intentions to act.

3. The Ideological Relevance, Success Factors, and Potential Impact on the Company's Image and Activities Need to Be Assessed Carefully. Ideological conditions are an important consideration. This is part of the reason why a top international Greenpeace leader publicly declared himself to be against the boycott of French products as a method of protesting at the time of the nuclear tests. In boycotting these goods, was one not perhaps denigrating the activity of French people who themselves were against nuclear testing? Moreover, what is a French product? Was it appropriate to harm an Australian manufacturer who produces French brands under license?

The risk is often not so much commercial (i.e., product distribution and sales) as corporate (i.e., image). It is nonetheless essential to prepare a mapping of the commercial risks run by the company's main markets.

The threat of an official boycott on the other hand is best handled by lobbying activities, whether under the cover of trade associations or not. European politicians' contesting the legitimacy of American laws imposing an official U.S. boycott on foreign investors in Cuba, Iran, and Libya showed that mobilizing elected representatives can still be a very effective weapon when the boycott is politically debatable and particularly when it looks like protectionism.

One very particular case is that of the double antagonist boycott. The classic case study is RU 486, the so-called "day after" pill from the pharmaceutical company Roussel-Hoechst. In this case, the company was the target of a boycott initiated by people opposed to the product being launched since they considered it immoral. It was then *also* threatened by a boycott of its drugs by supporters of abortion if the company decided to give in to antiabortion organizations and not put this product on sale!

V.   NEW RISKS AND NEW PRODUCT CRISES

Over the last ten years new crises have emerged as a result of new causes or conditions.

A.   Globalization of Production (Global Sourcing)

Many industries are currently affected by this kind of risk, particularly the electronics, pharmaceutical, food, textiles, and paper sectors. An accident or threat (be it social, governmental, or political) on a production site that supplies a large number of countries then exposes all these specific markets to a serious local crisis.

1.   *Marketing Strategy and Brand Image Are Jeopardized.*   There is a high risk of the product being discredited, stock disrupted, the corporate image being distorted, and doubt cast on standards and import regulations.

2.   *Corporate Communication Has to Be Perfectly Coordinated.*   It will have to cope at one and the same time with a global crisis and local national crises.

a.   *Any local production accident or incident immediately becomes international.* The mechanics of this globalization are through regulators (obligatory reporting to regulatory authorities such as the Food and Drugs Administration for example), the media (through press agencies and correspondents, world television networks such as CNN, main scientific publications such as Nature and Lancet), organizations (boycott calls, for example, by a multinational ecological or humanitarian organization or information exchange on the Internet) and politicians (for example, the European Commission taking a position).

b.   *Access to information about the cause of the accident is in practice extremely difficult both internally and externally.* Increasingly, manufacturing sites report directly to a distant decision-making center and are less and less under the control of national organizations in the countries where they are located. Local country managers are therefore only involved at a late stage because technical information is usually held back and corporate responsibility is internationally diluted or disconnected. In times of crisis, the "off-shore syndrome" always takes hold. The media besiege the site but the plant offers no communication; the national head office knows virtually nothing and therefore has nothing to say; the world headquarters remains silent; local production managers display paranoid reactions to both the outside world and the corporate group, suffering from feelings of blame or even fear, particularly where there are victims and/or suspicion of operational error or fault at the production site.

c.   *Contamination may affect raw materials from various sources and identifying the precise nature of the product risk is often impossible straightaway.* In most industrial sectors, the methods for tracing such materials are still insufficient.

d. A political or bureaucratic debate on the presence or absence of this kind of manufacturing site in the country may develop and turn rapidly into an argument. These days, global sourcing very often means relocation to countries where working conditions and respect for human rights are questionable.

3. The Problems Raised by Global Sourcing Do Not Only Affect Manufactured Products. The mad cow issue is a perfect example.

In this case, the raw material is quite simply beef and the global production source is not a plant, but a country, Great Britain. When it is not consumed as such, this raw material is used in feedstuff for animals and in numerous derivative products. The absence of reliable tracing methods and the lack of origin labels led to an international crisis affecting numerous products. Globalization developed mainly through regulatory and political routes (European Commission decision to ban imports of British beef), and the media (general and scientific press). It did not stop at the initial product but, through new scientific revelations, inappropriate analogy and rumors, affected other products such as milk, butter, cheese, and other animal species such as sheep, pigs, and poultry. The off-shore syndrome in the British government was a caricature of itself and highlighted criticisms of the split in political and administrative responsibility between Great Britain and the European authorities. The proposal to withdraw the product in question from the market entirely (in other words, the destruction of animals that were sick or at risk) created a serious economic, social, and political crisis.

B. New Market Positioning

Healthy and ecological positioning for mass-market consumer products (sugar-free, cholesterol-free, nitrate-free, phosphate-free, etc.) now expose manufacturers to as many marketing opportunities as losses of confidence. As a result, it is essential that the claim be strictly in line with the product's reality. Close scrutiny of scientific studies underpinning the pseudomedical promotion of certain food products leaves them looking thin. Applying the cradle-to-grave rule reveals without doubt that many *green products* do not currently pass the test of a serious eco-audit.

Doubts about a product's ecological qualities can give rise to a major crisis. The most famous in France is the phosphate war in 1985, which pitted Rhône-Poulenc, a European phosphate processor, against Henkel, a producer of zeolites, which were presented as substitute products in detergents.

C. *New Anthropological Trends in Western Society*

New anthropological trends condition the collective unconscious to accept or reject certain mass market consumer goods. They encourage the blossoming of many a social crisis taking the marketing of a product as both their justification and a vehicle for their communication.

1. Degradation of Medical Work and Scientific Expertise. This provides a foundation for disputing the effectiveness and safety of prescription drugs, liberalizing the regulations governing self-medication, and the marketing of parallel and traditional products with medicinal properties.

2. Humanization of Animals. The fight in defense of animals has led some of our fellow citizens to deny any justification for experiments conducted either to assess the safety of mass-market consumer products such as cosmetics or to develop new pharmaceutical drugs. This is a chronic and profound crisis of society in the West. Organizations that are these days constructed and operate internationally have not only been lobbying regulators insistently for many years, but now go so far as to call worldwide boycotts on products marketed by companies that have not given up animal testing. Some of the more extremist militant groups form real commandos, which do not hesitate to free animals from laboratories by breaking into animal houses at night and threatening researchers with death or even to act by sending them letter bombs. These activities always give rise to plentiful media coverage in the tabloids and popular newspapers.

3. North American Society Is Turning Back to More Puritanical Cultural Values. In North America, political correctness has become a powerful cultural and commercial filter. It can actually prevent the marketing of many mass-market consumer goods, or at the very least severely restrict their use in public. Unspoken public feelings about a given type of product have become the main cultural inhibitor for certain kinds of social behavior in the United States. In some cases, it has even taken a regulatory form. Smoking in public is the best example. The municipal council of a small town on the east coast has even gone so far as to ban its inhabitants from smoking on its streets!

NOTES

1.   Reward for the person who knows it before anyone else.
2.   The value of the Coca-Cola and Marlboro brands is estimated at more than 30 billion dollars (N. Dawar, INSEAD professor, "The Impact of Crises on Brand Equity." paper presented at *Les Echos* Conference, Paris, February, 1996).

2

Industrial Risk and Crisis Communication

I. MAJOR TECHNOLOGICAL ACCIDENTS

A major technological accident always generates the risk of a serious crisis.

A. *The Mechanics of the Postaccident Crisis*

1. An Accident Is Not in Itself a Crisis, It Is an Operational Emergency.   It imparts a huge shock to the structure of both the company and the organizations involved in managing such an event, seriously destabilizing their usual operating methods. In doing this, an accident exposes those involved in such a drama to critical questions about the value of their decisions and actions, the legitimacy of what they have said and even their behavior in the past, and sometimes even their very purpose and existence.

   2. Factors That Can Transform an Accident into a Crisis.   In our experience, crisis-generating circumstances always occur *in the same sequence* during the initial accident. To such an extent that, given our current understanding of the mechanics of crisis communication, it is now possible to develop a matrix for decision-makers that, in the event of an accident, will help them to anticipate successive scenarios and therefore prepare appropriate actions and responses to limit the permanent risk of migrating to a crisis.

B. *From Accident to Crisis*

1. The very first question people quite legitimately ask themselves immediately after an accident is, What happened? There is never a simple reply to this apparently simple question. In 99 percent of cases no one knows exactly what

29

really happened since the closest witnesses to the accident, those who were in the front line, are very often seriously injured or even dead. This key question is therefore generally asked at a time of great uncertainty about the cause of the event. It does, however, require someone to get up and speak for the organization since no one would understand if those in charge were to remain silent on this major issue. Revealing that one knows nothing about the initial nature or circumstances of the accident, however, would amount in the eyes of the public to admitting incompetence or, even worse, to suggesting that something inadmissible is being hidden. A detailed discussion of complex technical hypotheses incomprehensible to the average person would only be adding to the uncertainty and doubt, and opening a Pandora's box of arguments by experts of all kinds. In addition, any statement on what happened exposes the organization to delayed legal risk. This is why it is essential to phrase a very rapid factual response that is credible and understandable, satisfactory to both the media and the public, but in such a way that it leaves the field open to later and better-documented technical explanation. Following the explosion at Total's La Mède refinery on November 9, 1992, the announcement of a gas leak on the site was immediately perceived to be acceptable since it was a logical sequence to the event. When the response is not (or cannot be) phrased unequivocally, the accident immediately becomes highly suspect. This is what happened in both the TWA disaster on July 17, 1996, when flight 800 crashed just after take-off from New York, and the Eurotunnel accident of November 18, 1996.

2. *The scale of public emotions* aroused is in direct proportion not only to the scale of the accident and its consequences (victims, material damage, pollution), but also to the scale of media coverage, which varies as a function of several parameters including the visibility and profile level of the organization suffering the accident and the amount of news to be handled on that particular day. The same kind of technological accident may consequently pass completely unnoticed on the day that Gorbachev is overthrown or the Berlin Wall falls but, by contrast, make the top of the news in all media in a flat period such as summer vacation or the long Thanksgiving weekend. The cultural context and the symbolic value of the event are also factors to consider. A storm broke out in the British press, for example, following the fire in the Eurotunnel while the very same night the whole London subway system was paralyzed, trapping more than twenty thousand passengers underground! It has to be said that completion of this terrestrial border link between the island of Britain and the European continent has been a shock to the island mentality of more than one English citizen and that the accident did no more in fact than reawaken feel-

ings against the whole project. Whatever the cause, high-profile emotions are always treated dramatically by journalists and the headlines are therefore always very sensationalistic.

This emotional terrain offers very fertile ground in which the first organizational doubts may be sown in the form of criticism by the unions. Whenever there is a technological accident, layoffs, subcontracting, and a lack of training are the three key points of discussion that immediately appear in the media. Doubt also arises around management's intentions regarding reorganization and labor following an accident.

Against such an emotional background, a symbolic personality, the *survivor*, will appear, whose testimony will add to the emotional underpinning of the moment. The survivor who has miraculously escaped death is a mythological figure who touches the collective imagination and gives the drama its metaphysical dimension by illustrating the role of fate, an essential element of all human tragedy. Journalists, who know the power of fascination this type of hero can exert on their readers, do not hesitate to cross safety barriers to get an interview at the very scene of the accident, even to ambush the hero coming around in a hospital bed. As a result, for a few hours national or international media fame may be thrust upon any individual who was present at the scene of an accident. Someone who has survived may sometimes generate a collective feeling of injustice or of revolt—why are the others dead and injured, but not him?—or even attract the suspicions of the investigators—as was the case for the security guard who discovered and alerted the authorities to the bomb at the Atlanta Olympic Games before it exploded.

3. *After the emotions come the doubts, distrust, and arguments,* at a time when the inquiries (internal, government, legal) have only just barely started.

a. *The accusations target above all the lack of transparency in information* issued by the company and/or the public entities involved in the drama. "By not being totally candid and open, and by allowing doubts and rumors to spread, Eurotunnel took the considerable risk of frightening its future customers and disgusting its shareholders for ever," said an editorial writer in the daily *Le Monde* (November 24–25, 1996). What he was saying and repeating was that when a serious accident receives heavy media coverage, it is essential for a company, through its chairman, to commit itself solemnly to give full information to the authorities, its employees, commercial partners, investors, and the broader public.

b. *Distrust grows considerably when it turns out that it will be difficult or even impossible to find objective proof of the accident.* The black box recorder of the airplane has disappeared or is damaged; the refinery control room that contained the recordings has been destroyed by the explosion; the passengers' bodies and the remains of the fuselage are at the bottom of the ocean; the only witness to the fire has died of his burns. The thought that we shall never know the truth grows in public opinion and brings despair to the families of victims, who are suing for damages.

c. *In the case of an industrial accident, the theme of danger from pollution is another source of doubts* that very rapidly surface in the debate, particularly within local communities and among the media.

d. *The doubts that build a sense of crisis around the accident will focus on:*

- *Conditions leading up to the incident and its management.* Criticism generally focuses on the inadequacy of safety standards, on the functioning of detection and alarm systems, on the speed and quality of aid for the victims. In the Mont Sainte-Odile air crash for example, some people were astonished that it took four hours to find the wreckage of an airplane in France. In the Eurotunnel incident, a rumor suggested that it was a whole hour after the fire actually started when the British fire brigade was called in.
- *The future of the site, of the product, and of business.* "What Is the Future for Crédit Lyonnais?" was the headline in *Le Parisien* following the fire at the bank's head office. Forty-eight hours after the accident, they were still trying to determine the financial and commercial impact of the accident. How much is it going to cost? Who will pay? At this stage, confidence in a publicly traded company will translate directly into the share price. The financial consequences may also, in retrospect, appear very heavy for the insurance companies that cover the damage. If the economic implications are large, they may raise specific doubts among the victims as to the investigation's ability to ever uncover the truth about the accident.

4. *Three specific factors risk turning an accident into a crisis:*

a. *The revelation of precedents* is without doubt one of the most destabilizing factors. Not so much reminders of previous events that took place in the same industrial sector as similar events in the same company. Media files that contain a list of accidents at a company's plants and with its products are formidable. Everyone may understand that zero risk does not exist, but no one can understand why the same kind of accident can happen several times. The repetition of a similar accident on the same site or in the same industrial group (or sector) surely means quite simply, in the eyes of the media and the authorities, that no serious steps were taken after the first accident to prevent it from happening again! There is no escaping the media hunt for those responsible. One accident is bad luck, but several accidents mean something is seriously wrong.

Under such circumstances, there is a great temptation for the company to blame the accident on human error. Think twice before doing this. Bear in mind that blaming the driver of a train, for example, is an extremely serious accusation and that pointing to a scapegoat has become a less and less acceptable corporate attitude in the eyes of the public. In addition, the fact that a simple individual error can cause a disaster is particularly anxiety-generating since it clearly means that the safety systems are not capable of allowing for human deficiencies or foul play and of stopping their disastrous consequences in time. By contrast, the failure of automated and computerized safety systems meets with the public's favor. This type of explanation never fails, however, to reawaken instant union criticism of too small a labor force and a lack of training for the teams operating this sophisticated new equipment.

b.   Provision of both aid and compensation for victims.   The victims and their families have a voice and these days they speak loud and strong in the media. They form associations that systematically appeal for justice, a major contributing factor to the extended length of time crises can last.

c.   Accidents are frequently "globalized" by the media. For the most part, those who watch the news on television will live far from the accident so, taking Seveso as an example, the reporters will not hesitate to broaden the subject by focusing on the theme of regulation. "What is happening there today could very easily happen tomorrow near you." Simply showing a national map of the hundreds of such installations would be enough to attract the public's interest immediately and keep viewers throughout the country glued to their screens.

The media will naturally not hesitate, while awaiting the results of investigations and lawsuits, to recall the event on its anniversary each year.

II.   SETTING UP OR EXPANDING AN INDUSTRIAL SITE

A.   *The NIMBY (Not In My Back Yard) Syndrome*

The NIMBY (Not In My Back Yard) syndrome demonstrates that the technical quality of a project alone is not sufficient to win the local population's support.

It is essential to know how to win the greatest possible acceptability upstream of the project's implementation, not only by ensuring that it complies with regulations but by developing a realistic message and offering guarantees of transparency, nuisance prevention, and monitoring.

This body of information for local citizens on the protection of their environment in the context of economic development is governed by public inquiries. The problem is that they are often handled by inquiry chairmen whose average age is high and who are not up-to-date on the latest technological progress. By contrast, they tend to be particularly sensitive to the concerns of retired people, who want their heritage to survive and maintain its value.

The most frequently cited reasons for justifying rejection of a project are reductions in the quality of life, health, and safety of the local population. One tends to remember the highly symbolic slogan *Let Me Sleep* on a poster carried by a little girl protesting the establishment of a Worldwide Courier Express (DHL) air base.

Ecology movements find it easy to mobilize a certain stratum of the local population against an industrial project either by creating natural environment and regional heritage defense organizations from scratch or by using naturalist or local resident organizations that already existed as a core and bringing them back to life. These movements then repeatedly organize events with high media profile such as site occupations, residents' demonstrations, road or rail blockades, and petitions. They also know how to use or even abuse governmental and legal procedures.

The sensitivity of the electoral balance in some communities makes success easier for this process of communal dispute. In such a case, elected representatives are obliged to side with the opposition, often at the expense of not inconsiderable secondary economic and social advantages.

Objections from the public also embarrass the local authorities, who generally tend to sit on the case in anticipation of an assumed joint ministerial decision. In addition, governmental decisions are increasingly contested in the courts.

The regional press is by nature on the lookout for news items that will mobilize its local readers. Opposition to an industrial project (particularly if it is declared dangerous) is always a good subject for dramatic narration.

Major industrial corporations confronted with such a crisis tend to experience real difficulty in communicating with local populations:

- Corporate information on such a dossier is usually centralized at headquarters, far from local realities.

- The technical dossier is generally drawn up by engineers and administrators, whose jargon and technocratic presentation of industrial data already contain the germs of future community concerns.
- Support from a statistically based cost/benefit analysis is an approach that will have no effect on public opinion since the public tends to think in terms of all or nothing.
- The plant manager in charge of the case is usually an expatriate with no regional, social, or cultural credibility (the increasingly rapid turnover of site managers only worsens this psychological and sociological handicap).
- The timetable of formalities required by regulations only encourages leakage of confidential information and the dissemination of rumors in a provincial microcosm. Once the company is finally able to speak openly, defense organizations have already been communicating their case to the public for some time!

B. How to Communicate in Such a Crisis

Maximizing the chances for a high-quality industrial project means knowing how to do several things:

- Unravel the local situation by using an analytical matrix that is not only technical but also political, economic, social, and above all cultural. For example, the project to build a nuclear power plant in Brittany in a place called the Gates of Hell was obviously doomed from the start. Closing it without explanation and relocating it to the Bay of the Dead was no better!
- Create a climate of acceptability by developing a civic environment around the project. To achieve this, it is necessary to communicate on topics that can convince the population that the project on offer is the common denominator between general and specific interests.
- Change the technical details of the project. Environmental impact studies still too frequently expose projects to technical disputes that could have been avoided. The choice of service provider determines not only the quality of the work done but also its credibility. In addition, the presentation of an impact study must be understandable to all audiences. Do not hesitate therefore to use mass-market communication tools such as leaflets, brochures, models, and video simulations to explain the impact the project will have on the familiar environment as work progresses. Do not hesitate either, under certain difficult circumstances, to question the population directly

through surveys, to gain a better understanding of their concerns and need for information, and then to deliver it by direct mail, without intermediary.

III.   INDUSTRIAL WASTE MANAGEMENT

Waste has become a subject in its own right, discussed in newspaper and magazine articles, television reports, conferences, books, university reports, and even congressional sessions, as well as a political, economic, and regulatory challenge at the European level.

A.   *Household Waste Management Has Not Caused Many Crises.*

It can, however, become the subject matter for spectacular media coverage of a labor crisis. This has always been the case when refuse collectors go on strike in a major city since it generates widespread fear of the outbreak of an epidemic.

B.   *Special Industrial Waste Management*

This is a very sensitive area of communication that lies behind many crises in Europe:

- The storage and treatment of nuclear waste is a subject of concern, which seems to be gaining importance in the public eye over the dangers of nuclear power plants (excluding the very specific case of the plants in the Central European countries).
- Medical waste such as dressings, syringes, and radiography products have been in the news, particularly with reference to cross-border traffic.
- Chemical waste often presents sensitive problems ranging from the rehabilitation of industrial sites and safety in transport to packaging and treatment centers.
- The safety of special industrial waste destruction by incineration is still subject to criticism by some ecologists. Remember, in this regard, how the mad cow crisis revealed that the authorities were logistically incapable of rapidly destroying organic waste in large quantities.

3

Institutional Risk and Crisis Communication

Companies' positioning and corporate image have changed substantially in the social collective imagination over recent years. In Xavier Delacroix's words, hallowed by subsequent experience, "Companies that yesterday were only in the market must now operate in society" if they want to survive and prosper. They therefore need to build a relational matrix outside the closed world of their industry sector and traditional allies. Some of them are implementing communication strategies geared to presenting themselves as civic corporations, involving the development of humanitarian and social patronage.

Companies have slowly become aware (often at their own expense) that their employees are citizens (who vote), consumers (who buy their products but who also buy their competitors' products), shareholders (admittedly minority shareholders, but sometimes noisy and litigious), and even members of militant groups (ecologists). Managers in turn have become aware (often in brutal fashion) that shareholders are the real owners. As part of this general restructuring of roles, the major losers, in Europe at any rate, have without any doubt been the unions, who have lost their monopoly voice (and particularly hearts) in the political, economic, and social interface between corporate life and life in society.

Seen during the glorious thirties as a source of wealth and new projects for society, companies have turned in the public eye into sources of pollution, unemployment, and corruption. In addition, the European social fabric is currently undergoing profound changes. As a well-known judge, Laurent Davenas, so rightly puts it, we are in the process of "moving from a government-based society to an arbitration-based society." Judges have become the ultimate authority and have now, inasmuch as is possible, assumed responsibilities that are more political and managerial by making final decisions in matters of social protection, environmental preservation, corporate restructuring, and judgment of social representatives and politicians. Against a background of constant crises, it is therefore not surprising that an employee's commitment to his or her company's mission may have become very relative, even in Japan.

In an aging society where corporatism and regionalism are becoming more pronounced, unstable Western companies deprived of their public mission are looking for new corporate positioning in a world where the emergence of new markets has made them believe that they have an opportunity to escape from their political, economic, social, and cultural history.

I.   CORPORATE IDENTITY CRISES

Corporate identity crises generate labor and financial crises. In Europe they have taken a very particular turn with the recent increase of both privatization and chairman successions. These two situations touch the same sensitive chord: transmission of part of the national heritage.

A.   *Resignations and Successions*

Announcements of chairman successions are in plentiful supply in the press, which likes to name and shame "stars for a day" based on indiscretions, rumor, and dinners in town.

Resignations still too often resemble expiatory abdications. In a similar situation, the financial press is not soft toward these long-standing captains of industry, some of whom are now called gerontocrats, even though they have put their personal stamp on industrial development (e.g., in France, the United Kingdom, Italy, Sweden).

Resignations—Media Sequence The process generally starts some months before the planned departure of the chairman with the publication of the company's annual financial and social balance sheet. This is the ideal moment for opening a media file that focuses on criticisms, both financial and operating, of the company and its commercial strategy. It is not rare for rumors to start circulating about an early departure because of revelations to come, of accusations or an imminent investigation. In fact, it is quite simply the time for settling accounts. At this stage the chairman quite often grants a somemn interview in a major national daily newspaper, or is even obliged to appear on television, to reply to these accusations. This is the time for justification, which does not prevent confusion from building internally and sometimes marks a break with politicians and bureaucrats.

The departure, which always follows in short order, will help to mobilize some of the faithful supporters and allies, who will for one final time make positive statements to the media. In some cases, we have seen the chairman continue the struggle against the unions or the government right to the bitter end (the "last stand"). We have also seen a tendency to solidarity among his peers (as part of an advertising campaign) when the attacks have been too slanderous or when he has been subject to investigation or even imprisonment as power is passing to his successors.

At such a time, the press will always take the chairman's last message, which is issued in the form of a testament, while already speculating on the new state of affairs and what room for maneuver the new chairman enjoys. All that is left for the old boss is then to plunge resolutely into media obscurity for many long months or even years.

B.   *Privatizations in Crisis*

In both Western and Eastern Europe, privatization is the ultimate event that brings together all the ingredients of a serious crisis of social conscience and a national media thriller. The mechanics of the decision are opaque, there is a sense of loss of national identity within and outside the company, doubt is cast on the existence of a symbolic institution, national assets are sold to foreigners, small shareholders are victimized, and taxpayers are irritated.

Given this background, privatizations are high-risk political exercises from the economic and social communication standpoint. They almost always fuel the settling of accounts between captains of industry and political leaders, arouse feelings of rejection for employees (feelings of being sold off or betrayed), and even xenophobic reactions among the general public. All of these features are quite characteristic of a loss of control, which is in itself a pathognomonic sign of a crisis.

II.   MEDIA/LEGAL CRISES AND SCANDALS

The civil responsibility of company officials has caused much ink to flow and has caused many managers to be investigated. In France, four thousand complaints were lodged in 1994 against company managers following loss. Accusations generally refer to infringement of legal or regulatory directives, statute violation, or faulty management.

Scandals are actually quite different in nature. They include both flagrant personal enrichment and serious disfunction in very large and respectable industrial groups, traditional complicity between politicians and company bosses regarding the funding of political parties or to win re-

gional tender offers (*Capital* 1994). For some commentators such as Eric
Walther (1994), "The country is not dramatically more corrupt today than
it was yesterday. It is only that a squad of opinionated judges, a media that
is slightly less respectful than before and politicians' imprudence and im-
pudence have reignited a smoldering fire."

Judges and lawyers have now become real media stars. Daniel Soulez
Larivière (1993) has summarized this new sociological phenomenon
neatly:

> Over the last twenty years, social alchemy has created a new product, the
> media lawyer. A twin phenomenon seems to have taken place in justice and
> the media almost at the same time, completely changing the nature of rela-
> tions between justice and magistrates' secrecy and publicity. Under the tra-
> ditional system, with only a few exceptions, the police speaks, the judge
> maintains his silence, the press offers comment and the lawyer remains dis-
> creet. The journalist does the rounds of the police stations and court hearings.
> Nowadays, everybody talks, including the judge. Justice is played out on two
> stages, one media, one judicial, with a high level of interaction between the
> two. A suspect has to face an examining magistrate in the courtroom and
> twenty other examining magistrates in the media. Through its investigations,
> the media stage is sometimes instrumental in developments on the judicial
> stage. Even without such investigations, leaks from the judicial stage feed the
> media stage which as a result second guesses the judicial stage.

III.   INDUSTRIAL RESTRUCTURING

Industrial restructuring is always a long process that takes several months
in most of the European countries. It is always a difficult management exercise whatever the quality of the industrial, economic, and labor case,
given the legal requirements laid down by labor law on the one hand and
the human and social drama it often creates on the other. Existing regulations force the corporation to be flexible, requiring much patience, good
knowledge, and considerable management expertise in local psychological, social, and cultural factors if negotiations with employee representatives are to be successful. There is, moreover, a whole legal arsenal of
weapons that can hinder, delay, block, or cancel the process. Resort to external auditors, tribunal decisions, regional and national media, symbolic
action on sites and on the public highway is quite usual. Direct appeals to
shareholders, customers, and suppliers are also frequent. Nowadays representatives use these events as personal media grandstands and the public authorities are increasingly ambivalent about taking positions. As a re-

sult, during negotiations everything can hinge on the social plan. It is no longer uncommon for the judge to turn it down and the company to be forced to rewrite it, which can cause delays of several months.

Industrial restructuring in Europe is always a risk for both corporate and brand image. That is why one of the key corporate communication targets is to limit the operation regionally, inasmuch as is possible and to avoid a national political or social debate.

A. The Scale of the Crisis Is Closely Linked to Political and Social Factors

In Europe, given current difficult labor conditions, any industrial restructuring immediately assumes a political dimension. The scale of the shock depends not only on the number of employees affected by layoffs but also on the majority shareholder (domestic or foreign company), industrial sector (public service or private enterprise), and the type of operation (relocation, privatization, or sale).

1.   Relocation and the Sale of a French Company to a Foreign Group Are Two High-Risk Kinds of Industrial Restructuring.   Any relocation of industrial expertise considered part of French industrial heritage is an open invitation to all the emotional outpourings inspired by xenophobia. This is not an exclusively French phenomenon. The purchase of Rolls Royce, the ultimate British status symbol, by a large German group whose name means "people's cars," triggered fairly heated media and social debate.

2.   The Restructuring of National Companies Is Always the Subject of Major Media Crises.   In such cases, the central theme for the unions is the protection of public services and the preservation of national independence. Restructuring is particularly badly received internally since it is often the prelude to privatization. Under such circumstances, crises are often both general and very regional at one and the same time, since restructuring casts doubt on the company's, or even the industry's, very reason for existence and also dismantles historical provincial sites. Their magnitude means that local communities experience them as real social and cultural shocks, which for many years exacerbate imbalances in national economic development. Mobilization in reaction to this can be very powerful. In such a typically highly explosive situation, corporate communication by the companies involved is unfortunately still too often managed clumsily and even incoherently, given the very narrow room for maneuver and negotiation available to management teams, particularly when they are under direct political influence.

B. *Possible Crisis Scenarios Are Quite Stereotypical*

- Union criticisms claiming that there is a lack of consistency in the company's industrial strategy.
- Strike calls, or at least actions to block or delay production and product distribution.
- Physical confrontations such as imprisonment of one or more members of the management team on site; employee demonstrations or parades through the town; temporary blockading of neighboring roads; and occupation of production sites to prevent the moving of machinery.
- Anonymous threats, even individual criminal action, such as blackmail threatening product contamination.

C. *Factors Contributing to the Magnitude of the Crisis*

- When the restructuring takes place at a time of year that is helpful in mobilizing unions or the media, such as during an election period, just before the long summer vacation period, or in the fall, when people return to work after their vacation.
- When the brands marketed by the company are foremost in the collective imagination.
- When the sites involved in the restructuring are very close to the capital or some other major urban site. Local interest makes national media coverage by television stations easier.
- When the company restructuring is part of the fiefdom of a local elected representative of national political importance (for example, a current cabinet member).

D. *Factors Tending to Reduce Political or Media Mobilization*

- When the industrial sector is considered damaged in public opinion or if it has enjoyed too many privileges for many years.
- When the reduction in employee numbers affects mainly management executives and few or no wage-earners. (The solidarity between these two socioeconomic groups may however vary.)

E. *Company Management of Communication during Restructuring*

It is essential that a company that is going to restructure design a global communication strategy in close collaboration with lawyers, social restructuring experts, and communication consultants.

1. There Are Several Basic Principles.   Any public relations activity related to high-profile events or promotions should be discreet or even suspended throughout the restructuring process.

- There should be no product or corporate advertising on television during the week of the announcement.
- Sales should on the other hand be managed in the usual way. In particular, sales team meetings should continue to be held and are vital for motivating staff and counterbalancing any rumors.
- Financial communication should be managed with the restructuring in mind. No one can ever understand why there are layoffs on the same day that good results or even exceptional profits are presented to shareholders.

2. There Are Powerful New Trends   In Europe judges are becoming the latest guarantors of a social model. Judges continue to monitor social plans very closely and are even venturing into new territory. They now pass judgment on companies for "not having a strategic plan or budget forecast" or for "a lack of training to help employees adapt to changes in employment with a view to keeping them in the company." Frédérick Lemaître (1996) questioned this trend in an article in *Le Monde*:

> Unions' resorting to the legal system may be a consequence of the complexity of the law, but it does of course amount to a failure not only of management but of collective bargaining and indeed of the unions themselves. Since they are often incapable of mobilizing employees and establishing a critical mass of followers among employees, unions look outside the company for the support which they no longer command internally. . . . Whether we want it or not, ten years after the removal of government approval for layoffs and faced with the ineffectiveness of collective bargaining on employment matters, judges have now become one of the final guarantors.

In reaction, some bosses are now rebelling openly in the press against the judges' intrusion into their social plans and certain decisions involving companies' payment terms.

- Political and social discussions tend to become more radical when the company has a strong presence in the region. A high level of employee and regional representative mobilization in 1996 led the French government to reorganize its social plans in the arms industry, put off SNCF (the national railroad) reform and to suspend privatization of the state-owned banks.
- "Grumblings by public bosses" (Delanglade 1996) faced with politi-

cal decisions that are poorly explained or not explained at all in Europe. Managers of public corporations are normally required to show reserve and allegiance to authority as government servants. Today, however, they increasingly speak out against autocratic decisions and practices that they contest. Strongly worded statements by them in the media then force the authorities to make embarrassed official corrections or to make irritated comments or even draw verbal threats from ministers whose authority has been questioned. Journalists no longer hesitate to consider such disobedience by public bosses to be a duty, while others even speak of legitimate defense. Some even go so far as to compare them with human shields.

IV. FINANCIAL COMMUNICATION IN TIMES OF CRISIS

An *Entreprises & Médias* working party has established types of financial crisis, including:

- The announcement of a fall in earnings.
- A negative rumor about a company's financial health.
- A change in major shareholder and the threat of takeover.
- Opposition to a financial transaction by minority shareholders.
- A sharp split in the company's management team.
- Withdrawal of a key product from the market.
- A major operational accident.

These events take place against an economic and institutional backdrop undergoing significant change. Publicly traded companies are de facto international and must, as a result, communicate in the world's leading financial markets. Hard cores of shareholders are becoming increasingly soft and traditional alliances among owners will not much longer withstand the logic of world markets. Pension funds and insurance companies will question the national pension systems in Europe and their employment benefits. Some American so-called "ethical investment funds" do not hesitate to question publicly the conditions under which companies operate in certain nondemocratic countries.

The lowest common denominator in this type of situation is the negative impact on the company's share price. This is why it is essential, in times of crisis, for a major industrial group to take mandatory reporting of information to stock market operators into account. "It is very important . . . to disseminate . . . the same information at the same time to the company's various audiences: internally, to the press, to financial analysts and to those responsible for selling shares to institutional clients in the dealing rooms of the main financial market intermediaries" *(Entreprises & Médias)*. It is also important to be in a position to monitor investors' reactions directly on Reuters or Bloomberg screens. It is at times like these that the true worth of a company's corporate reputation in the eyes of the financial markets can be assessed.

V.   INTERNAL CRISIS COMMUNICATION

A.   *The Principle of Communicating Vessels*

Any external crisis affecting an organization always has major repercussions internally. This is why communicating with employees should have top priority in a crisis.

Internal crises may develop for a period of time within the inner sanctum of the company, and then suddenly become external through media revelations. By (sometimes inappropriate) analogy and generalization, they can then affect a whole industry sector or even become the subject of debate in society. Sexual harassment is a case study of this kind.

B.   *Sexual Harassment*

In the United States, sexual harassment has gone from being a simple news item and now causes major corporate crises or even scandals.

The biggest case of sexual harassment in the private sector grew out of a complaint lodged in April 1996 by hundreds of women at the American subsidiary of Mitsubishi. Sylvie Kauffmann (1996) reports that, according to a representative of the Equal Employment Opportunities Commission (EEOC), female employees worked constantly in "a climate of fear and vulnerability" and were faced "daily with all sorts of harassment, being treated as whores and sluts, subjected to being touched inappropriately by their male colleagues, finding pornographic comments about them at their place of work, being refused promotion if they refused certain sexual favours." Nearly five hundred employees are said to be involved in this scandal, which might in the long run lead to the payment of damages that could total nearly 150 million dollars.

Other companies such as McKinsey and Booz, Allen & Hamilton also face legal complaints.

Public services have not been spared this kind of scandal either. Everyone can still remember the televised confrontation in 1991 between Anita

Hill, a young academic, and judge Clarence Thomas, a candidate for the Supreme Court, whom she accused of having harassed her. This broadcast immediately unleashed an unprecedented wave of claims for sexual harassment.

In the United States, crisis has also affected the army, where women are admitted into active service. The latest official statistics lament the frequency of rape at 4 percent (*Newsweek*, November 25, 1996).

This social phenomenon is a media and legal subject that has crossed the American border. The AVFT (European Association Against Violence Toward Women at Work) records two hundred cases each year. In July 1996, the European Commission decided to consult social partners on the problem since legislation was considered inadequate and the member states had managed to transpose the Community's 1991 recommendation on protection for men and women at work only very partially into domestic law.

Close-hand communication to family, friends, and colleagues, and combat communication to lawyers and unions are the two customary routes the crisis takes, bringing an internal secret out into the light of day.

Management of such a crisis often results in negotiated dismissal. It is important to note, however, that increasingly today the accused publicly refute the allegations and counterattack legally or even through the media, stirring up internal and external arguments that in the long run always tarnish the company's overall image.

4

Major Collective Fears
and Crisis Communication

Twelve years ago, Jean Delumeau (1987) wrote:

> Throughout a community's history, fears change . . . but fear remains. Man is engaged in a permanent dialogue with fear. We are therefore constantly striving to overcome either old or new fears which threaten to paralyze us. Is that not what we are currently experiencing? . . . Our fellow citizens do not really live in fear of another world war. That seems impossible to them since it would amount to collective suicide by mankind, but here they are now, confronted by fearful and invasive unemployment, insecurity heightened by terrorism, pollution caused by damage to nuclear power stations and chemical plants, a fierce offensive by cancer and the growth of AIDS.

Since then, cows have gone mad, the hole in the ozone layer has grown in size, the earth has quaked and destroyed Kobe, algae have invaded the Mediterranean Sea, students at our schools and colleges are breathing in asbestos dust, and we are told that the next generation of pensioners will be tomorrow's new poor. Not to mention the Millennium Bug. . . .

This is the overall media background redolent with permanent fears, against which the increasingly isolated individual seeks reassurance about his or her fate.

I. TERRORISM

A. *Terrorism Is Either a Media Phenomenon or Does Not Exist*

Terrorist movements "need the media to give their actions the greatest effect, or more exactly the greatest publicity," as L. Huberson has remarked. The crucial problem in today's show business society is that between free publicity and democratic information, journalists' room for maneuver has narrowed considerably. In the face of terrorism, they have "no manual, no instructions" stated television director, Jean Drucker (1977), in perfectly good faith. In such a situation, manipulation and disinformation are permanent threats.

We can as a result lament with Patrick Lagadec the ascendancy of the all picture-based culture—which creates specific risks related to the direct dissemination of sensitive operational information and which trades in horrible and unbearable pictures of victims in defiance of their most basic rights and the suffering of the families who see them.

Information is broadcast in the name of a media mindset that guarantees journalists the right to impunity, amnesia, glory, and money while the drama lasts. Today the speed with which information is transmitted is directly proportional to its commercial value, so it is not surprising that a scoop always wins out over contemplation. The demands for total and immediate media coverage have also become a top priority right in the collective unconscious, which demands pictures from the height of the drama on the "box." The general public follows police searches like a real television series and live executions are now often the final scene.

B. *Institutional Messages Are Very Stereotyped*

Government messages are, of course, intended to reassure the public about the measures that have been taken in an effort to limit terrorist actions and their dramatic consequences as much as possible, such as a special plan where the army is called out to protect vulnerable and strategic points or borders are controlled with identity checks on public roads. Political communication in a crisis aims in spectacular fashion to show a worried population that in such a situation the government remains determined and firm.

For the opposition parties it is, of course, the right time to express their solid stance on the issues as well as their attachment to the defense of republican values while remaining vigilant about the nature and length of the measures that might affect the free circulation of goods and people or even cause xenophobic reactions (judging by appearances).

The purpose of institutional communication is essentially to gain time and help investigators make rapid progress, away from indiscreet observers, in their search for those responsible, and to end up if possible by dismantling active networks. Unfortunately, pressure from public opinion and the media does not allow politicians to remain silent on institutional matters for very long, particularly if there is another attack. As a result, the publication of information that casts doubt on the work of the investigators is both frequent and damaging. It is too often disclosed to journalists through both blunders and indiscretion, manipulation, or disinformation.

C. *Communication between Victims and Aggressors*

This has been treated in many studies, particularly those dealing with hostage-taking.

The first few hours are always extremely critical and are particularly unstable if there are many wounded, sick, dead, or young children because this only contributes to collective anxiety. The nature of communication behind closed doors between victims and aggressors is to a large extent dependent on the number of people present and whether or not weak hostages are allowed to be evacuated in return for logistical benefits or agreement to move. Note that spontaneous leadership is easier in a small group of victims and in turn makes it easier to codify communication with the aggressors better. In a bigger group seen as more difficult to control by the aggressors, it is more common for instructions to be radical and behavior more extreme. In such a case, hasty executions are an immediate fear.

After several hours together in the crisis situation, a gradual trend to empathy may develop, potentially resulting in some understanding or even complicity between victims and aggressors. This is known as the Stockholm syndrome, described in 1978 by F. Ochberg following the hostage-taking in a Swedish Credit Bank on August 23, 1973. This paradoxical behavioral process and the psychoemotional response have since been confirmed regularly in many incidents.

Trained terrorist commandos have drawn lessons from the Stockholm syndrome, as psychiatrists have observed:

"Periodic replacement of guards who must remain masked with hoods when facing their prisoners, as little as possible verbal exchange, very harsh conditions of imprisonment and rough physical treatment if not brutality are all designed to eliminate the risk of any emotional exchange which might at any moment turn positive" (T. Bigot and A. Féline, in Dormont, Bletry, and Delfraissy 1989).

Revolutionary commandos use the Stockholm syndrome for media propaganda ends by releasing hostages who come around to supporting their cause, in minute but very effective doses, as was the case when hostages were taken and held at the Japanese Embassy in Lima, Peru some years ago.

II. MAJOR HEALTH FEARS

Major health fears are part of collective memory. Among their number are counted plague, leprosy, cholera, and tuberculosis. In our modern world, the media, international by nature, has without doubt helped to give a disease such as AIDS the image of a planetwide sickness and has even created irrational fears of the whole human species being in danger (Ogrizek, Guillery, and Mirabaud 1996). The social and political effects of this are severe: medical stigmatization and marginalization of whole social groups and exclusion of sick people. This institutional self-defense reflex has unfortunately not changed very much over the centuries, particularly since the discovery of new contaminating agents has in recent years reawakened fears of epidemics. These include exotic viruses such as Ebola and Marburg, atypical micro-organisms such as listeria, and infectious proteins like prions. In addition, the fact that traditional germs are now becoming resistant to antibiotics, which has had much coverage in the media, has done nothing to reassure people.

Major technological risk and ecological concerns have created new health fears such as leukemia and cancer, related to the chemical and nuclear industries. We now worry about the emergence of atmospheric pollution–related illnesses and the development of diseases related to our way of life and consumer behavior. As a result, medical rumors run rife, including the connection between cellular phones and brain tumors, aluminum and Alzheimer's disease. It must be said, however, that with the passage of time, products in common use a few years ago, and still generally present in our food, houses, and even in our bodies, such as additives, asbestos (Mayle 1996), and silicon, have now turned out to be dangerous to our health. Therapeutic risks are also the subject of many medical or legal news items or even international scandals, such as contaminated blood (Morelle 1996).

The general consensus is that we have played sorcerer's apprentice in many areas relating to our ability to control life. The mad cow scandal represents a fundamental epistemological break in this respect (Hirsch, Duneton, Baralon, and Noiville 1996).

Future major health scares will no doubt originate mainly from biotech products. This is a field rich in fantasies. The marketing of genetically modified soya is already the subject not only of spectacular disputes by ecology groups such as Greenpeace, but also of commercial resistance by distributors and central buyers. The publication of irrational articles on the subject (calling it "mad soya" or "Frankenstein food") has only fueled the panic, doing nothing to calm people down.

5

Communicating in a Crisis

One can easily put together a list of some twenty features ranging from control to responsibility to transparency, to show the attributes of what could or should be a good way of communicating in a crisis. In a real crisis, however, no one can actually achieve such ideals. Perfection is impossible given the speed of events, the complexity of the situation, the stress level, the large number of uncertainties, and media pressure. Those who have experienced several crises know that it is modesty that is needed more than anything else.

On the other hand, it is possible to apply several principles whose effectiveness has been proven by experience. The hard part is managing to apply them simultaneously in an emergency.

I.   MAJOR PRINCIPLES

A.   *Move Fast*

Speed is without doubt a determining factor for successful crisis communication. The questions raised are often distressing, but waiting too long to react is seen as a sign of weakness or confusion.

That does not, however, mean that speed should be confused with haste. Avoid wanting to explain everything, say everything, and answer every question immediately. The very minimum required is to give basic information very quickly, together with the essential facts, while indicating what measures have been or are being put in place.

In order to move fast in an emergency, the first prerequisite is not to lose any time. There are endless reasons for losing time, including delays in getting internal information; hesitation; procrastination; reporting complexity; divisional separations; anticipation of further information and certainty, which will often only come much later; lack of precise procedures or those calling for too much approval by superiors; communication systems not operating as planned such as telephone exchanges not working, an emergency room not being equipped, documents not being accessible, or lists not prepared; excessive perfectionism in drafting press releases that say nothing more than what everybody already knows.

In practice, in order to avoid all these snags, emergency facilities need to have been planned and if not developed in detail then clearly defined with clear internal information procedures including who tells whom, responsibilities designated in advance including who does what, and premises designated with the minimum equipment required. This should make it possible, at the very least, to be operational quickly.

Moving fast in communication means managing to inform various parties in the first two hours, including the media, governmental authorities, local representatives, local residents, business partners, and, internally, employees directly affected as well as managers who will be affected later.

B. Anticipate the Medium Term

The outbreak of a serious incident obviously calls for decisions and action in the very short term. It is essential, however, that the whole crisis unit does not find itself wrapped up in a group of problems relating to that precise moment or to the very short term. An instant review of possible developments over the next few hours or days is a top priority of crisis management since crisis is by definition a dynamic process. The initial incident, be it an accident or other, consists of a number of facts that will develop over time. Examples include:

- Technical control may be exerted quickly but may also encounter difficulties.
- The number of victims may increase, become more complicated, or even become distressing for the general public.
- There may at first appear to be no impact on the environment, until the realization that there actually has been damage.
- Hostile reactions, accusations, and revelations may emerge after a few hours.
- Implications—political, economic, or social—that were not apparent at the outset may emerge after a few weeks.

In principle, it is necessary to consider all these developments, which will considerably change the profile of the event. Anticipating developments through scenarios in this way is also applicable to the well-known sequence of phases always seen as a crisis unfolds.

C. Be a Credible Source of Information

Everybody accepts that accidents can sometimes happen, given the volume of operations like production, distribution, and transport, and that a particular combination of circumstances can overwhelm preventive measures. Tolerance of the accident depends a great deal, however, on the quality of reactions to it when it happens. It is hard, for example, to accept that the company in question might not give out reliable information, as one would expect of a responsible organization. This can quickly become unacceptable, particularly if the information turns out to be suspect, too incomplete, or even false. Such behavior can destroy the trust that might have been put in the company. Journalists (and other interested parties) will go looking for information elsewhere and in the days that follow may tend to doubt any new information given out by the company.

It is therefore essential, if one wishes to have and to keep the trust not only of the media but of all actors in the event, to be a source of reliable information. This assumes that answers be quite precise, complete, coherent, and credible, qualities not easy to achieve in practice. In an emergency, the reliability of the first information gathered is actually quite delicate. Assessing the facts may in itself be tricky and several sources are usually sought by the media (or give their views spontaneously), both outside and inside the company. Inconsistencies, which raise doubts, may therefore develop very easily if one does not immediately adopt a strict structure of internal communication and coordination among the entities involved, i.e., the company, the authorities, the emergency services, and the experts. The ideal is to be able to speak with one voice. Inconsistencies within the crisis unit may be avoided by identifying a single and sole point of entry and exit on each of these fronts to manage the information flow.

The Eurotunnel fire on November 18, 1996, offers a striking illustration of inappropriate communication, featuring immediate claims in the aftermath of the accident that the safety system was effective and that services would restart quickly. In fact, it turned out the next day that the fire had been much fiercer than announced, that there were major safety problems, and that no services would be able to resume until after a long period of costly work. This led to vicious denunciation of the company's "lies" in the media.

D. Be in Step with Perceptions and the Nature of the Event

Public opinion and the media never experience crises by objective scientific criteria. How could that be possible? How could the public affected approach a safety or health risk in a rational way at the very moment when the risk has just been dramatically revealed with reports from the first victims for them to see on television? Under these circumstances, it is essential, when putting in place appropriate forms of communication, to analyze and take into account the emotional and sometimes symbolic aspects of the risk raised.

When these two major factors are combined, it becomes ridiculous to base communication, as we far too often see, on misplaced technical comparisons or statistical arguments.

Similarly, it is absurd to count on measures that are unsuitable, considering the very nature of the risk in question.

In the mad cow scandal, following disclosure of the risk that the disease could be transmitted to people, the VF [i.e., *Vache de France* ("French beef")] logo was not in itself reassuring (even partially) to French consumers. The logo actually conveyed a collective statement about the quality of French beef while at the same time one could see suspect herds being slaughtered in Côtes-d'Armor and learn of fraudulent imports of foreign beef. In addition, the VF stamp on French beef was also, ironically, the initials for mad cow in French (*Vache Folle*), only adding to the general confusion!

E. Put the Crisis in Perspective

In a crisis, the company should take a position on the issues by stating its fundamental corporate values. What is the real problem that threatens the company?

In the Airbus A320 crash on Mont Sainte-Odile near Strasbourg, for example, what was the real problem for Air Inter: the reliability of its aircraft (considering precedents), having two pilots (a collective bargaining issue), the lack of GPWS alarm (approved by senior civil aviation managers), or complete responsibility for the victims (only possible by renouncing the Warsaw Convention)?

In the Josacine case, was Rhône-Poulenc Rorer's priority problem knowing whether this was an isolated or a serial incident (in the latter case, investigations would inevitably be long) or, whatever the possible scenario, preventing at all cost the death of another child (which would involve recalling the product and informing parents of the extreme emergency)?

In a crisis, managers must act in line with their company's ethical values, and send the public a clear message about the corporate position and their priorities. The complete withdrawal of a product from the market sends a clear signal that consumer safety is the company's top concern, whatever the financial and commercial consequences.

F. *Respond Immediately to Accusations and Confusion from Guerrilla Communication*

Even more in a time of crisis than a time of peace, silence is consent. Rumors, arguments, doubts, and accusations are never in short supply in the days that follow an incident. If the company involved does not respond rapidly (in a reasoned way, not just with simple denials), public opinion, which has been sensitized by the emotion and by the expectation of more information, will interpret silence as acquiescence.

Confusion, which is only encouraged by the media when they listen to views from different people, can also rapidly obscure or even ruin a company's policy of transparency. Have no fear, therefore, to explain, in a basic manner and with simple diagrams if necessary, the technical features of the problem, particularly safety procedures and equipment.

G. *Mobilize and Coordinate Internal and External Resources*

In a crisis, mobilizing internal resources is far from common, even though the need for it would seem to go without saying. A tendency has been observed among managers to turn inward, compounded by a desire to protect a confidentiality that is in any case illusory. This attitude is, without exception, inappropriate. It can even be rapidly counterproductive since it will inevitably cause delays and errors in the implementation of desirable action. To the contrary, it is preferable to search out in advance the company's skills and human resources, based on clear information and with confidence in the potential for mobilizing staff in times of difficulty. Experience shows that, under these circumstances, employee involvement is generally excellent. It is also a good idea, in line with a strategy of having allies (preferably organized in advance), to think to call on outside resources including trade and corporate partners and experts. By speaking out, they can substantially reinforce the credibility of what a company is communicating.

H. *Instigate Actions That Can Influence the Course of the Crisis*

The role of communication must not be limited to the dissemination of factual information, with some messages and explanation, or to the development of consistent and credible responses. What is more important in a crisis is the ability to think up and instigate actions capable of having a positive impact on the crisis itself, either because they are geared to responding to doubts or uncertainties, or because they have a strong symbolic value in offering reassurance and in displaying the company's commitment, responsible attitude, or even its desire to be transparent. Do not hesitate to be proactive in an emergency. It is always a good idea to announce immediate measures of support or protection just when the emotion of the incident is at its peak.

Less than two and a half hours after the bomb exploded at the Port-Royal RER (suburban line) station in Paris on December 3, 1996, the RATP (Paris rapid transit authority) began to introduce a campaign of posters, stickers, and badges bearing the catch phrase "Alert, together," and including detailed advice for travelers. The transport authority also invited travelers to show their support and their understanding by sporting a sticker (widely circulated to subway users). Such an initiative, truly a case of crisis communication, deserves commendation. Another example is Air Inter's decision after the Mont Sainte-Odile crash to introduce special arrangements for full compensation of victims.

When it comes to symbolic gestures, however, it is crucial to make commitments only to actions that are completely convincing. When the president of the United States takes his wife and daughter to visit the Three Mile Island nuclear site shortly after the accident, he is demonstrating his political and personal commitment to the unequivocal statement that there is really no more risk. A civil servant, on the other hand, who nibbles a leaf of lettuce to prove that the Chernobyl radioactive cloud has left no fallout in his area, or Tony Blair PM, who declares that he eats genetically modified food, can only offer a very small amount of conviction.

II.   DEVELOPING SCENARIOS

A.   *Potential Negative Effects of an Incident*

This method involves exploring the potential negative effects of an incident by asking two key questions: What if? and What next?

This exercise generates a future vision of the incident and its impact, and prevents the predicament of getting stuck solely on the immediate aspects. It also helps to anticipate arrangements and steps that might be needed—because they are reviewed as part of the exercise—and the responses that might have to be given since they will already have been formulated. Having imagined possible negative developments and prepared oneself for them also leads to a much more strategic vision of how to manage the situation. Consideration of the negative results that might arise helps to avoid getting trapped in positions that are too simplistic, too assertive, or too optimistic at the outset and that might then cause bitter disappointments and reduce credibility. This method also helps to escape *groupthink*, or "a behavior pattern in which individuals who are deeply involved in a highly cohesive group, work extremely hard to remain unanimous within the group rather than to achieve a realistic review of possible lines of action" (Janis 1982).

This dangerous process particularly affects management teams that are strongly united under a charismatic leader or are simply very tired. It develops into an "illusion of belonging to an elite and invulnerable group" in the face of adversity. Members of the crisis unit then close themselves off in one-way trains of thought, systematically censoring themselves and overrationalizing the situation in too stereotyped a manner. "In this way, intelligent and even brilliant men are led to make unanimous stupid decisions resulting in a fiasco" (Janis 1982).

B. *Designing Technical Scenarios*

Decision-makers usually respond well to the idea of designing technical scenarios to anticipate preventive measures in the field. Other scenarios should, however, also be considered. These concern the victims, social representatives, consumers, the media, and the government. For each situation it is possible to create a list of the players who will be affected by the incident and to imagine their possible negative reactions, both immediate and delayed.

C. *Applying the Scenario-Generating Approach*

In practice, applying this scenario-generating approach is a specific crisis unit task.

Two people should be given the responsibility by the unit manager to close themselves off periodically and consider possible developments. As hastily improvised as this technique may appear, in a crisis it is very effective, helping to gain several hours in the implementation of preventive measures.

D. *The Attractions of the Scenario-Generating Method*

The attractions of the scenario-generating method are not limited to acute incidents such as accidents.

In any potential risk situation it is actually very appropriate for managers to look in principle at worst-case assumptions and developments. The main difficulty is psychological. Organizations reject alarmism. It has, however, been established that forecasting and preparing help considerably limit difficulties if the worst does materialize.

Though not the first, the mad cow crisis offered a spectacular illustration of this situation. On March 20, 1996, the British minister of health announced ten cases of Creutzfeld-Jacob disease in humans, probably related to the bovine spongiform encephalopathy that had affected 160,000 cows in Britain over the preceding ten years. It then became clear that the worst-case assumption, i.e., that the contaminating agent could be passed from animal to people, had never really been considered by the authorities. No plan for communicating in a crisis such as this had been considered. Worse still, specific scientific research into prions had apparently been discouraged by the authorities and no diagnostic test had been developed to identify sick animals that would have simplified protection measures considerably.

In fact, nothing had been prepared at all, so communication with the public on this everyday and potentially major risk was then completely improvised with the consequences we now know.

III. COMMUNICATING WITH THE VICTIMS

A. *Victim Management*

Victim management has become one of the major challenges, if not the central challenge, of crisis communication (Filizzola and Lopez 1995).

The impact of such management on the image of the organization or corporation (and sometimes the whole industry) concerned is always significant and often considerable, not only immediately but in the near and distant future as well. Unfortunately, there are a very large number of examples from crises in recent years that demonstrate this fact. Simply think of silicone breast implants, air crashes and hijacks, the contaminated blood and growth hormone affairs, and asbestos. In fact, whatever the crisis, the problem of the victims has always been in the foreground and still is after several years. Conflicts, claims, denunciations, and legal battles have followed one another and continue to do so, most often legitimately, it has to be acknowledged. In truth, the subject is often apparently a question of compensation. The important point to stress, however, is that the victims' and/or their families' core demand is for the truth about the causes of the incident and legal acknowledgment or attribution of responsibility. This demand finds powerful echoes and powerful backing in public opinion.

It is clear that there has been very sharp sociological change over the last ten years. Was the essential driving force the contaminated blood scandal and the thousands of hemophiliac and transfusion victims? Perhaps. The trend is very broad, however, and victims today are constantly banding together quickly and forming defense organizations. Their role has been very important since several among them have been particularly active, and rightly so, in demanding legal recognition of victims' rights.

Note also that media coverage of victims' demands has become systematic. Each demonstration, each commemoration, and each press release are reported in both the regional and national press. These actions frequently give rise to further reporting where the victims express in detail the reasons for their anger and their fight: refusal to provide information, promises not kept, compensation inadequate. These are all opportunities to revisit the facts, recall the doubts, and once again highlight the attitude of the corporation or organization in question.

On the other hand, in more general terms, the media regularly echo consideration of or plans regarding changes in the victims' status. Several themes have developed recently: the need in medicine to recognize a right to compensation, even where there is no fault (therapeutic risk legislation); the importance of a medical and psychological assistance in an appropriate way, including when there are no physical injuries (as is the case for witnesses to terrorist attacks); involvement of specialists, from the earliest moments, to see that financial assistance packages are put in place quickly and that the question of compensation is dealt with immediately; changes in legislation on corporate bodies' criminal liability.

Today large parts of the public are certainly sensitive to these themes. Everybody feels that they or their loved ones are potential victims of a terrorist act, a medical accident, or a public transport accident, even a technical accident or a natural disaster, and it seems fair to everybody that under such circumstances society should be able to react more quickly, provide better information, designate clearer lines of responsibility, and take more complete responsibility for victims and their families. This current of opinion is very strong, to the point where sociologists have been able to say that a "victimization of the individual" phenomenon is developing in our modern society.

In any event, in practice, the pressure on this issue of victims is still strong and emerges quickly when there is an accident, whether the effects appear suddenly or gradually. The attitude of the corporation affected is always under scrutiny through much media attention, and any possible failures are immediately highlighted. These will without fail give rise to questioning, even to insinuations that remain in the collective memory and are recalled at the slightest opportunity. It is essential to understand this process and of course to try to avoid it through appropriate communication. In order to achieve this, several basic rules must be applied to crisis unit operation.

B. *Taking the Victim into Consideration*

The victims must be taken into consideration as quickly as possible. This assumes that within the unit, from the start, there will be a competent responsible person for whom victim management will be the sole and specific role. This person will have the ability, planned in advance, to mobilize the necessary human resources to organize coordination of information (with rescue teams on site and with the other players in the incident) and to direct all aspects of communication.

The problems that arise are often difficult to handle, starting with the question of identifying victims. The first few hours, particularly in the case of technical and transport accidents, often involve major uncertainty in this respect. The same can be true, however, under different circumstances, e.g., food or pharmaceutical product contamination or equipment failure that may lead to physical accidents.

Know also that in a crisis the concept of victims is not limited to physical victims, either present or potential. Several people (or groups of people) who would not necessarily come to mind immediately may have suffered or fear suffering more or less direct damage. Such is the case for local residents near a plant when there has been an explosion or fire with an escape of fumes that may be toxic; for fishermen if water pollution threatens; for customers whose interests may possibly be hurt; or for members of staff who may be worrying about their jobs.

The key principle underlying communication with and about victims is proactivity. This means anticipating as much as possible any action to provide information or assistance that might be timely. Giving information to families, for example, is an absolute priority. It must be early and if possible active, e.g., setting up a toll-free number, organizing information meetings, and even a reception unit are strongly advised, together with urgent training for people capable of giving credible responses. Better still, it is pertinent to be able to announce immediate assistance measures. This principle does not only apply to accidents. It is also true when a potential problem arises regarding the use of a contaminated or dangerous product.

Communication with victims and families absolutely must be appropriate to their very specific psychological experience. In other words, it is essential to take account of stress and distress. These are clear in the case of death, injury, or disappearance or when the circumstances of the accident are by their very nature extremely traumatic such as community disasters, fires, shipwrecks, or terrorist attacks. It should, however, also be acknowledged that victims exist when there is no serious damage and where objectively the risks are low. Professionals such as doctors and psychologists will, of course, be able to give precious assistance in preparing information. Do not hesitate to ask for such assistance.

Generally speaking, experience shows that many communication errors are regularly committed through failure to make real and full allowance for the particular psychological experience of victims or their families. It is essential to understand that under these circumstances a company's initial attitude sets the tone. Any information deficit and even any clumsiness will only increase victims' stress, distress, or disarray. This can be neither forgotten nor forgiven.

C. Material Assistance and Compensation

Material assistance and compensation must be considered quickly. Considering the specific legal aspects and insurance implications, this is certain to present complex problems. It is, however, desirable in all cases to commit oneself as soon as possible to actions that first and foremost meet ethical considerations. Here too, it is recommended that specialist assistance be sought from victim support schemes. They have precious experience in setting up the appropriate systems. It is also recommended that the most appropriate contractual terms be agreed in advance with insurance companies for any incidents that might cause damage.

D. Monitoring Victim Management

All aspects of victim management demand regular monitoring in the following weeks and months. It is not enough to have provided the right flow of information during the first few hours and days after an incident. Information on the progress of investigations and compensation procedures in particular should be provided actively and with the greatest possible transparency. Victims and their families do not want to be forgotten while several of their questions still remain unanswered and they have consequently not been able to start the mourning process. Communication therefore continues to play an important role at this stage and it is preferable to face up to difficulties, of which there are generally bound to be some, rather than to close up in a silence that will always be interpreted as evasion or withdrawal.

IV. INTERNAL COMMUNICATION FIRST

Whatever the crisis, the same observation always holds. Managers focus almost obsessively on the media and government authorities and completely forget (where it is not a case of refusing in principle) to pass information to their own employees. These employees hear the information from television news bulletins in the evening or by opening their newspapers in the morning. This lack of internal information also very often continues over the following hours and days.

Such an attitude is clearly totally inappropriate in a crisis. First because employees are often the first to be affected by the incident, both directly, where their personal safety is concerned (if, for instance, they live close to the site or are users of the products), and indirectly, since their skills, their ethics, or their jobs may be in question. Employees are moreover often the main spokespersons outside the company. They face questions from industry partners, the media, local representatives, and their family or friends.

Bearing in mind the fact that a crisis always undermines the factors that make up corporate identity such as "feelings of belonging, value, autonomy, and confidence" (Mucchielli 1993), the initial lack of clear information for employees will be an impediment when it comes time to ask for their support and mobilization.

As we can see, everything points to how important it is to set up early internal communications. Added to this is the fact that a lack of internal information flow brings major risks. An inevitable failure to understand the situation leads to displaced, incoherent responses and attitudes among employees. Frustration at not having been kept informed generates reactions of distrust, demotivation, and resentment, which can persist for a long time. Rumors, generally negative ones, develop about the circumstances surrounding the incident, managers' reactions, delays in measures taken, and long-term consequences. It is clearly preferable to avoid all these damaging effects since they may go so far as to create truly calamitous situations.

This form of communication should not be limited to the initial phase of the crisis. Employees should continue to receive information about the situation's development and particularly about the victims (especially if they are employees), the outcome of actions taken, and planned measures to limit the consequences. Finally, in some cases, particularly accidents, it is a good idea to bring together several internal levels of seniority to discuss and learn from the experience.

V. CRISIS COMMUNICATION AND THE MEDIA

A. *"It's the Media's Fault!"*

It is true that the media love crises and corporations hate them. It is also clear that media coverage is one of the essential factors transforming an incident into a crisis. It is therefore not surprising to see the media reproached for the way they outbid one other or offer simplifications, approximations, interpretations or value judgements and sometimes even quite simply for their description of reality! In a crisis, a corporation always feels a certain sense of being under attack or even of injustice. Managers generally believe that journalists are looking systematically for sensationalism, cannot understand the technical and scientific problems, say anything, never check anything and, above all, are uncontrollable! "It's the managers' fault!" the press then replies, believing that companies never say everything they know and hide the truth, and that at the end of the day profit comes before everything else.

B. *Media Operating Methods and Crisis Communication*

1. *The media's sophisticated communication methods go hand in hand with the most extreme cottage industry.* Anyone who has visited an editing room will agree. It may be true that planet Earth has become a media village and that the press agencies work in real time, but it is also true that one person's news does not necessarily interest others and that many journalists still very often depend on secondhand information, particularly outside major urban areas.

2. *Media coverage of a dramatic event will depend on many factors.* In particular, the nature, scale, or cause of the incident, the time or place it happened, the quality of the victims, and how well-known the company is. In a crisis, and throughout its development, the most recent information is what provides the reference point for media messages. This is the information that journalists will want to grab. As a result, it is quite common for details to become headlines, opinions information, comparisons analogies, and rumors facts. One of the factors determining the importance assigned to an incident is the competition's attitude. An item that is a lead story in one paper will not be left out by other publications for long.

3. *The crisis will be managed by very different journalists over the course of its development.* In the beginning, freelancers, beginners, juniors, and columnists will write the first reports. Specialists might add their comments later. Then, as the crisis expands, the big names will appear on the scene.

That said, by virtue of their business, journalists acquire the habit of working to urgent deadlines: "being organized and making decisions quickly with an acute perception of time. . . . They are used to the unexpected since due to the variety and suddenness of the items they deal with, it is their daily fare" (L. Huberson).

C. How Companies Cope with the Media

To blame the media or believe that reason and good sense are the commonest things in the world is to expose oneself to major media risk. Similarly, to neglect the impact of the press on public opinion would be to seriously underestimate the impact of "It's in the paper" and "I saw it on TV" in today's collective imagination.

In a corporate crisis some bosses of major industrial groups still too often believe that direct pressure on journalists and managing editors is the best method of counterattack, along with going to court (i.e., arbitration). It must be acknowledged that this has been known to work, which raises the delicate issue of freedom of the press, but it is also important to understand that when silence is broken by a leak or the relationship becomes unbalanced, the media fall will be that much harsher for both the manager and his team.

In a major technical crisis, "the company too often takes cover behind technical press releases which give a deplorable technocratic image under circumstances where human dramas are center stage in the media" (Lagadec 1993). When communicating with the media, the five Cs offer a desirable course to follow: concern, clarity, control, confidence, and competence.

D. Prepare for Media Exposure

This is indispensable in the modern world. Preparing means on the one hand understanding the media mindset, where "nothing is true and nothing is false; there are only alternative points of view" (Lagadec 1993). On the other hand, it means accepting the idea that "there are no bad questions, there are only bad answers" (Oscar Wilde). This requires:

- Preparing managers to act as spokespersons in front of the media (particularly television cameras).

- Being a continuing and reliable source of real-time information.
- Knowing the journalists who write about the industry and establishing relationships of trust.
- Knowing the company's media record, i.e., all the significant media events or archives that have affected the company in the past.

VI. SYMBOLIC COMMUNICATION

Symbolic communication is a strategy very often used by politicians, organizations, judges, and the media. It has been neglected, however, by industrial groups for both corporate and crisis communication.

A. *Definition and Objectives*

Symbolic communication consists in openly taking a position that can be seen as an example by public opinion. It aims to channel and crystallize individual emotions to open the way for collective awareness. To operate in symbolic mode, this position must be part of a so-called disruptive strategy, i.e., a dynamic in which there is a break with the background context and flow of events.

B. *Impact on Public Opinion*

In a crisis, symbolic communication is always more powerful in its effect on public opinion than any rational technical argument. Symbolic positioning of the challenges on emotional and moral ground is always more effective in mobilizing public opinion than presenting a position that is politically, technically, ecologically, and legally correct. Symbolic communication can, however, be a double-edged sword. In the words of Michel Rocard (1996), "Symbolizing all the factors which have become a difficulty or a problem, one after the other, will only make the solution more difficult to find and intensify the conflict. . . . Symbolic emphasis . . . precludes subtle compromises, slow developments and gradually developed solutions."

C. *Stage Management*

Public opinion must initially be confronted dramatically, in the theatrical sense of the word, with the corporate position.

1. *That may mean a simple presentation, a single gesture, individual act, or collective event.* Take General de Gaulle's June 18 appeal, one man's lone confrontation with a tank in Tiananmen Square in Beijing, and the "white march" in Brussels the day after the judge in the Dutroux affair resigned.

These are all examples of powerful symbolic communication in times of crisis.

2. *For symbolic communication to be successful, the shock of photographs and the weight of words (or silence) are not enough.*   The event must be given a corporate significance that both heightens the emotional gearing and transforms the emotion.

The photograph published after the gas cylinder exploded near the Maison-Blanche subway station in Paris, several hours after Khaled Kelkal's funeral in the Lyons suburbs, for example, was a close-up of a bolt on the asphalt with a chalk circle drawn around it. This photograph on the front cover of French newspapers encapsulated not only the intense emotion generated by the sight of the murder weapon, but also reflected, symbolically, the circle of police investigation tightening around the terrorists.

D.   Symbolic Risk

1. *Social and cultural signals are often hijacked in images and analogies used in symbolic communication.*   Flags, embassies, historical monuments or sites, tombs, logos, abbreviated names, signals, posters, and advertising films are all targets and provide material for militant symbolic communication.

2. *Mass-market consumer goods or high-profile goods (real or virtual) also suffer the same fate.*   There are many examples of this: clothing (the Muslim veil), money (U.S. dollars), food (beef), drinks (Perrier), drugs (Prozac), service (air traffic control). Some are already corporate symbols—Champagne and Beaujolais Village for example as well as chlorine and CFCs!

3. *Politicians or mythical characters are preferred targets for demonization.*   For example, Bill Gates or Saddam Hussein.

4. *Some events are symbolic by nature and offer opportunities for symbolic militant action.*   Examples include official visits, commemorations, or anniversaries. Similarly, in the industrial world, the end of a chairman's term (the eve of his eviction or a successor taking over) and takeovers are events with high symbolic potential.

E.   Classic Vessels for Symbolic Communication

1. *Direct Material.*   There are many of these, found in most street demonstrations. They include disguises, masks, streamers, blimps, balloons, pamphlets, posters, graffiti, pins, and brooches. Everyone remembers the red ribbon used in the anti-AIDS campaign. Sometimes things can be hi-

jacked from their original function with humor to reflect symbolically an unusual crisis situation. Workers striking at the Bigard de Quimperlé slaughterhouses in Brittany, for example, marched in diapers to protest being forced to take bathroom breaks at set times!

2. *The Media.* When it comes to symbolic communication, the media prefer direct reporting, caricature, photography, big headlines, editorial and viewpoint articles, which can of course be used for the publication of corporate advertising inserts.

a. *Caricatures are formidable symbolic communication tools in a crisis.* They often make people laugh but also incite them to reflect on the underlying issues. As a result, everyone wants to pass them on. The international press will not hesitate to swap them and reproduce them. All major incidents are subject to symbolic pictorial parody.

b. *Symbolic corporate advertising inserts.* This is a method used increasingly by major corporations that experience a major crisis but do not succeed in consistently conveying their message in the media.

c. *Multimedia and the internet.* The information superhighway is used increasingly to convey symbolic messages.

F. *Symbolic Communication Tactics*

There are four major symbolic communication tactics used frequently in crises today:

1. *Media Commando Raids.* This is a technique involving confrontation and contesting of claims. Roughly, it goes like this: Having called together a group of journalists (particularly television reporters), a small group of militants stages a surprise occupation of a site and remains in occupation as long as possible in a sit-in or die-in or by chaining themselves to each other. Alternatively, the group disappears very quickly, having caused damage to stop the site's activities. As a general rule, streamers and/or a press release demanding action are included.

The purpose of this tactic is to impart a shock. The medium chosen for broadcasting the event is television. Images convey emotion and are by their very nature national and international. To be arrested by the forces of law and order or to be pursued in court helps to pad out the emotion and the debate in the public eye or even in some cases to win rulings favorable to the cause. Militant organizations such as Greenpeace, Act Up, Pro Life, and Peta are well trained in this kind of symbolic action.

Other situations involving confrontation and contesting of claims can also become platforms for symbolic crisis communication. These include hunger strikes covered by the media, church occupations, children's demonstrations (which were "normal young kids" in the Dutroux affair in Belgium, but parades of mongoloids in the case of anti-abortion demonstrations).

2. Media Coverage of Lawsuits   This tactic is very effective given the current media and legal culture. It involves obtaining either a ruling in or the blocking of a corporate case in progress, or the dramatization of a debate in a public place.

Note one characteristic that reflects current standards well. With increasing frequency, journalists receive information on the filing of a suit before the legal authorities do! Inquiries, investigations, and lawsuits are all becoming useful platforms for media visibility.

3. Media Sacrifice   The aim of this technique is to eliminate the original cause of the crisis, e.g., by withdrawing a defective, suspect, or dangerous product from the market and stopping production, regaining the initiative in terms of communication, and restating the corporation and its managers' ethical stand by setting an example. It will not, however, be effective in the public eye if it is seen by *vox populi* to be inadequate or too late and when it is poorly communicated. It may be contested, which will only worsen the crisis when it is seen as inappropriate and/or disproportionate. As a result, this tactic should only be deployed when it is quite appropriate.

The typical symbolic human sacrifice is a manager's resignation. There are other well-known forms of symbolic human sacrifice including the fall-guy in major technological accidents or the scapegoat in political or legal affairs and also in society's crises.

4. Solemn Institutional Commitment in a Crisis Can Be Expressed in Several Ways:

- A handshake in front of television cameras. This might for instance mark peace between two countries or between two men, signifying the end of the crisis.
- Request for support (possibly with the publication of a corporate insert in newspapers).
- Boycott calls are one of the classic symbolic communication techniques of humanitarian and ecological organizations (with petitions and direct correspondence to company chairmen).

Symbolic communication is therefore a tactic with high strategic potential in a crisis, both outside the company and internally. It is, however, very hard to implement for industrial managers who are not at ease with the emotional dimension and still wish to reassure the public with rational technical arguments.

6

Crisis Unit Organization and Operation

Companies, government organizations, and the media have developed the habit of applying the term *crisis unit* to any emergency management meeting following a serious accident or conflict. This meeting is often presented as being called to discuss solutions, make decisions, or adopt arrangements geared to crisis management.

This overextended use of the term leads to confusion about the very nature of a crisis unit. It is a specific entity whose role is first and foremost operational (otherwise it would be no more than a discussion meeting between various managers or partners). There is confusion also about the objectives of this entity. It is there to ensure coordination in making decisions as well as acting on several fronts including logistical and technical management of the incident, and communication management at all levels, both internal and external, where necessary. In the case of an accident, some of the actions are led *in situ* by a so-called local control station positioned as close as possible to the incident. The purpose of these preliminary specifications is to attract the attention of those who want to set up a crisis unit and to establish suitably equipped premises and an ad hoc procedure. It is better to avoid making mistakes at the very beginning of the unit's structure and function. A crisis unit is intended more for action than discussion.

I. UNIT ORGANIZATION

A. *Unit Meetings*

The first item to plan is details of unit meetings in an emergency. This is a real problem, particularly for periods outside working hours such as nights, weekends, and vacations, which are often involved. The simplest approach is for each member of the unit to keep current personal details for all the others on a card on his or her person at all times. A telephone number for conference calls will help to establish contact between several people rapidly, to share information, and to assign and initiate the first actions, even if they are only aimed at obtaining more detailed information and warning those who have not yet been informed. Obviously, the person designated as director in the emergency procedure, or his or her replacement, should make the decision to call an immediate meeting of the unit. Unit member access to the premises at any hour of the day or night needs to be formally arranged with the local security services.

B. Premises

For high technology risk companies or organizations that may have to manage major serious incidents, special infrastructure is required, specifically designed for the coordination of substantial and complex technical and rescue operations. Communications facilities need to be particularly effective (see P. Lagadec's well-documented works on this subject). In all other cases, it is sensible to opt for quite simple facilities, which may even be adapted from existing premises. The important thing is to have several rooms close to one another. These should include a large room, e.g., a conference room, with an adjoining room, preferably separated from the first by a partition and a glass door. The large room will be the incident room, where all cell members can meet, particularly for checkpoint meetings. The adjacent room will be the communications room with faxes and telephones. Secretarial offices should be close by with computers and photocopiers. Also close by should be two or three offices that can be vacated so that unit members can be in peace by themselves to think and write.

C. Telephone Facilities

Ideally there should be a special crisis switchboard in the communications room. Calls can then either be transferred from the main switchboard either automatically or after initial filtering. Alternatively, calls could come through directly from individuals to whom the number has been given such as outside company managers, governmental authorities, rescue services, and business relations. These facilities make it possible to handle telephone calls more quickly and in a more organized fashion and are extremely precious when there are lots of calls. With a trained secretary running this crisis switchboard, many calls can be managed on a preliminary level and routed to the right person without disrupting the functioning of the unit.

It would also be ideal to have the communications room be partitioned into open units to which calls can be distributed from the switchboard. It is also practical to have direct lines, one or two into the incident room itself, others into adjoining offices.

In some dramatic situations where a company risks being literally submerged with calls, it should not hesitate to relocate and install batteries of telephones and faxes.

D. *Posters*

Large amounts of wall space for mounting posters in the incident room itself and in adjoining rooms is also a major priority. It is important to be able to stick up, and therefore visualize as on a radar screen, a large amount of information, i.e., not only plans and diagrams, but also posters and tables listing the names of victims, facts, actions, people to contact, and responses to be delivered.

E. *Reference Documents*

All basic documents regarding company procedures, sites, activities, and products (particularly plans and security files) should be gathered together and regularly updated in a large cabinet in the incident room. The same is true for all technical data and catalogs, guides, or listings that may have to be consulted in an emergency. It is also recommended that several files should be drawn up containing information on previous history, security, and environmental policy, as well as activities with key figures. Computerization of this data helps to reduce space considerably.

F. *Audiovisual Equipment*

It is essential to have at least a radio and a television set with video recorder since the crisis team needs to be able to listen to and watch live media coverage of the incident in real time. Press agency despatches should also be reviewed in real time. It is therefore important to have direct access to terminals such as the Associated Press, Reuters, and Agence France Presse.

G. *Catering*

In times of stress, the need to eat and drink must not be neglected. A refrigerator, microwave oven, and coffee machine in a room adjoining the incident room must be considered basic equipment.

II.   UNIT MEMBERS AND THEIR ROLES

There is, of course, no ideal model for a crisis unit since incidents requiring such management differ significantly from one industrial sector to the next as well as by type of incident.

A well-constructed crisis unit can be fully operational with eight or ten people in some cases, along with other colleagues on call in the field and in various departments to apply action and delegate tasks. In other cases the unit will have to involve a larger number of managers when their presence is made essential by the number and complexity of priority actions. There are, however, a number of constants in the functions that have to be fulfilled, making it possible to establish a kind of central core or basic setup that holds true for almost any unit. This can then be adapted and built upon as necessary.

Unit Director.   The director must be unambiguously designated in advance depending on the main incidents considered in the emergency plan. He or she has two roles: unit operational management and decision-making and strategy. When it comes to the unit's operation note first that the director will usually have to be very forceful, particularly in the establishment and running of checkpoint meetings, the composition of small working groups, compliance with methodology, and drawing up of documents. In order to fulfill this strategic function, the director will have to remain detached, maintaining a global perspective of the incident and the way it is developing. He or she will have to be able to withdraw from time to time, in consultation with one or two unit members, to define or redefine objectives and priority actions. *A deputy director* will be able to help in monitoring the unit's smooth operation and in reorganizing task sharing as needed.

Operations Manager.   In liaison with the local control station, the operations manager initiates, directs, and coordinates all necessary technical actions, whether it is a matter of containing pollution, recalling product batches, or evacuating people.

Logistics Manager.   The logistics manager directs the mobilization of all rescue and communications resources that are to be put in place externally. This person is also responsible for all the equipment needed for the unit, such as offices and adjoining rooms, catering, and reinforcing of secretarial and other resources.

Security Manager.   The role of the security manager is to plan for all aspects of the incident that might have an immediate or future impact on people, be they employees, local residents, or consumers, installations, and equipment.

Environmental Manager.   The environmental manager plans for the possible impact of the incident on the natural environment and takes any useful steps to avoid or limit such damage as much as possible.

Internal Communications Manager.   The role of the internal communications manager consists of identifying, listing, implementing quickly, and monitoring all necessary and appropriate steps to disseminate information within the company. This includes sites affected such as production or distribution facilities, the various managers, services, and entities concerned such as switchboard operators, marketing department, or international subsidiaries, and the internal skills to be applied.

External Communications Manager.   The external communications manager is responsible for anticipating the priority communications actions needed, depending on the incident. This applies particularly to the media, since they may become involved very quickly, and local residents, local politicians, the authorities, and other players in the crisis.

This manager prepares such communication by drawing up as quickly as possible a brief giving the company's position on the incident and, with the assistance of other managers in the unit, a first question and answer document.

The position brief should summarize the basic factual information, the company's position, and measures taken (in collaboration with the rescue services and the authorities). This essential document will serve as the basis for drafting press releases. The external communications manager also monitors the reactions generated by the incident, both in the media and elsewhere, in real time and on a continuous basis. He or she passes this information on to the unit at checkpoint meetings and develops the question and answer document in the light of these reactions. This manager is also responsible for briefing the company's spokespersons.

Victim Manager.   Any crisis involves the concept of either actual or potential victims. The role of the victim manager will be to identify and anticipate all aspects of this problem. He or she will design and implement any flow of information and assistance required.

Legal Manager.   The legal manager should be proactive in considering all the legal aspects of the situation in the immediate and medium-term future, particularly the problem of responsibility and relationships with subcontractors. He or she approves all reports that are issued and makes certain that all important actions can be substantiated. He or she works together with *the risk manager.*

General Secretary.   The general secretary is active in establishing the time line of the crisis. He or she also provides his colleagues with a table reminding them of actions decided upon but not yet implemented.

Secretaries.   In a crisis it is absolutely essential to have secretaries whose availability is planned and who are trained with the unit in crisis procedures.

Depending on the situation, various other people, such as assistants and managers capable of handling specific tasks, will be seconded to assist the crisis unit's work. Management will also be able to call on *outside experts.* The important thing is that all the necessary actions identified be carried out in coordinated fashion and as quickly as possible.

III.   WORKING METHODS

Let it be said straight away that working in a crisis unit calls for almost military discipline. Unit members need to move fast, handle a large amount of information, and carry out several coordinated actions while at the same time retaining as much as possible their analytical and decision-making capability. It is not possible to work in a team unless behavior, role, and speaking time are controlled. The aim is not to operate automatically, but to benefit from the considerable gain in time and energy made possible by applying some order and certain methods. With P. Lagadec (1993a, 1995), we should recognize that a unit that has not been well trained has little chance of giving satisfaction in a crisis. Several methods that have stood the test of experience are particularly effective in a crisis and are worth using, whatever the initial type of incident.

A.   A Time Line

It should be an automatic reflex to establish a time line. This is the role of the unit's general secretary. This management document will be essential both from a legal and an experience standpoint. It must be as complete as possible, including all significant information and actions with precise timings.

B.   Checkpoint Meetings

The technique of checkpoint meetings is really the backbone that makes it possible to structure and operate a crisis unit. Do not hesitate to call these meetings systematically every hour or even every half-hour at the beginning. They must by definition be short, lasting about five to ten minutes, and review the situation quickly on its various fronts. The objective, and this is essential, is that each member of the unit must have the same level of information at all times. Technical and strategic discussions should not form part of these meetings—they take place elsewhere. Without checkpoint meetings, increasingly substantial gaps develop in the flow of information within the group and particularly between technical members and communications managers. Coordination becomes impossible and inconsistencies develop.

C. The Question and Answer Document

This consists of a rapidly drawn up list of twenty obvious questions that all interested parties are going to ask and, in note form, responses gathered from each manager in the unit. The whole thing should be typed, reread, approved by the director, and distributed. This document should then be regularly updated. Without such a document, the organization is inevitably exposed to improvised, incomplete, and inconsistent answers given to different contacts. If the crisis continues, this document will help those who take over to have a written record of what the company initially said.

D. The Scenario Method

Applying the scenario method is just as essential in an emergency as in times of peace. Not using it is to be condemned to being simply reactive and at the mercy of events and repercussions. In such a situation, it may be possible to manage the incident but certainly not the crisis that risks resulting from it.

E. Real-Time Review of Media Coverage

A crisis almost always attracts very substantial media coverage with a rapid succession of press agency despatches, radio flashes, and television reports. Very quickly, this media coverage will include reactions and comments (and sometimes doubts) from a large number of players, as well as questions and/or statements from journalists who will have a sharp influence on the public's perception of the incident. The response of the company involved is picked up more or less clearly and completely in the first flow of information broadcast.

It is therefore a good idea to gather these factors without delay and analyze them to manage them as best as possible from the communication standpoint. The initial image of an incident always sticks in the memory and conditions all subsequent media coverage.

IV.   MANAGING THE POSTCRISIS PERIOD

A crisis is not a closed system, it is open-ended. Other phases follow the acute phase, the incident itself, and its immediate consequences, and a break in the flow, which is what constitutes a crisis, constantly risks setting in. Nothing will ever again be quite as it was. This particular postcrisis period must be taken into account and managed even if the media have fallen silent and things seem to have returned to normal, even if the crisis has apparently been well managed, and even if there is a great temptation to close the case and move on.

Several actions, involving communication, can be considered.

A.   The Voice of Experience

It can sometimes be painful to draw lessons from a crisis. It is better, however, to do so sooner rather than later. Thought should naturally be given to the technical lessons that are always essential in correcting or improving any facilities, rescue services, or resources that may have been defective or inadequate. Efforts should also be made, however, to look again at the various stages of the incident, not forgetting the run up, and analyzing them in terms of crisis management as such. Where and when was time lost, were difficulties encountered—which precisely?—or were methods or resources lacking? A complete time line drawn up during the crisis will make this review easier.

This does not mean wallowing in a series of personal self-criticisms. On the contrary, this should be avoided and the focus put instead on factors that came into play: delays in information or assessing it, for example; imprecise emergency procedures; confusion between decisions and communication; inadequate internal communication; or mobilization of the corporation's human resources. These are all diagnostic tools that will help to strengthen the crisis unit emergency facilities' organization and operation.

B.   Evaluating the Impact of the Crisis

The impact of the crisis outside the organization can vary enormously depending on the circumstances. It is important to distinguish the short-term impact from the medium-term to long-term impact. A crisis that appears well-managed in the short term may have very destabilizing consequences for the corporation affected, which only become apparent one or two years later, e.g., the Perrier crisis. This is why it is wise to be modest in making a priori judgments of the management of a crisis whose full details and implications are not known.

In some cases, there are objective signs such as falling visits or sales. Quite often, however, there are no such signs. It is therefore a very good initiative to conduct opinion surveys on the perceptions of the incident, the risk raised, and the company's attitude, in the eyes of the relevant public, be it trade or consumers. The results of these surveys will considerably help communication. For example, if the company's attitude is generally understood and approved, it is easier to stay on course, despite arguments, to explain what has not been understood or to reinforce a given message. All of this information will also be useful when planning to start up again, whether it be recommissioning a plant or putting a product back on the market.

A more sensitive point to consider and manage is the impact of the crisis inside the company. This is in no way parallel to the external impact and is often neglected. It is, however, not rare for internal experience of a crisis to be dramatic, particularly if the incident involved victims, if corporate ethics have been called into question, if the decision has not been understood, or if the incident further exacerbated conflicts between departments or even between managers. This can be profoundly destabilizing as a result, even if it is not very apparent or very much expressed. There have been real implosions that started insidiously with extended unease over several months or years. Combined with this go dissatisfaction, doubts, resentment, fears for the future, and rumors. These are exacerbated by the lack of clear and effective internal communication from senior management who get to the point where they never again want to hear about the incident. Quite the contrary, ways should be put in place, and quickly, for both management and staff to express their thoughts, through information meetings and an expansion of procedures for lessons to be learned from experience.

C. *Monitoring of Actions*

From the very day of the incident that triggers the crisis, several types of procedures and actions come into operation. They unfold over several months or years and include internal, government, and legal investigations as well as the assessment of damages and compensation. Technical management of these procedures is, of course, a matter for specialists with the relevant skills. Do not forget, however, that these various actions form part of the crisis itself. Questions of insurance are often subject to media coverage, as are victims' actions, such as setting up defense organizations or making claims, together with preliminary inquiry results, be they official or not. It is also desirable for the crisis unit not to let such factors as these, which can prolong the crisis, develop without managing them and working out an internal and external communication strategy. On the contrary, it is sensible to anticipate them and be proactive.

D.   Vigilance

One crisis can lead to another. It is not uncommon for a second crisis to develop in the days or weeks following an incident, having been hidden or stirred up by the first.

Following the revelation of one failure or fault, others may be sought and found. Acute pollution, for example, awakens interest in chronic pollution. It may also occur to observers that the problem raised could apply to other sites or other products, or that it is worth addressing in a much more global way. Other possibilities include the fact that the crisis, by virtue of the questions it raises, has revealed structural weaknesses whose resolution can no longer be put off; or the crisis has initially awakened an attitude in the minds of community representatives and other business relations that will have to be offset in the long run. All of these quite classical mechanics should be anticipated by the crisis unit.

Attention must also be paid to possible deferred questions and doubts in the minds of experts or organizations such as trade or consumer associations, which may continue to mobilize long after the original incident.

The possibility should also be systematically considered that a further incident of the same kind might happen, such as another accident or new product fault. Even if it is not serious or less serious, if such an incident were apparently similar to the one that caused the crisis it would be a major risk. It would automatically lead to the particularly dangerous suspicion of repetition (a repeat proves that the measures announced have not been introduced or are not adequate) and will reawaken arguments and disputes with renewed media coverage. Communication should then be immediate and particularly convincing to avoid analogies and prevent doubts and accusations from arising without a response.

Finally, recurring media coverage should be considered, once again systematically, particularly on anniversaries ("It has now been one year . . .").

Controlling the postcrisis period therefore includes, as we have seen, a whole process of preventive management and communication that is as important if not sometimes more so than during the acute phase. That is why the crisis unit should not be designed to be exclusively devoted to emergencies. For an organization or corporation, a crisis unit is an operating entity that must remain operational over both the medium and the long term. This does not mean that a dozen managers should be permanently on call to deal with a "ghost issue." Regular, quite short meetings are generally enough to ensure that the problems of the postcrisis period can be managed. Above all, it is a question of establishing a mindset and a feel for the method. The stakes, from both the image and the financial standpoint, fully justify this investment.

7

Training and Preparing for
Crisis Communication

Why and how is an incident already an instant crisis or does it become a crisis? Are there relevant criteria for determining this? Do crises have the same specific and particular characteristics such as a common process or constant aspects? Is it possible with some training to acquire expertise that can become operational at such a time: What is the best way to work in a crisis? What organizational structure and resources need to be deployed? What methods should be used?

The answers to all these questions are now well-known to many consultants who, based on sufficiently broad experience, specialize in crisis methods and management, particularly for industrial crises. The bulk of this experience can also be effectively passed on to motivated company or organization managers through theoretical training, which can be concentrated into a few days. There is no sense to this training, however, if it is not put into practice in the form of absolutely essential drills.

I. CASE STUDIES

From an educational standpoint, the most lively and appropriate initial approach to understanding the mechanics of a crisis is without doubt case studies of real crises. This is based on an examination of successive media coverage of the incident. When the media do not themselves cause the crisis to erupt (which happens sometimes, but less often than thought), they will in any event relay it and concentrate virtually all of the significant information. After the initial incident (which may itself not have been covered by the media) there are few important episodes forming part of the crisis that are not sooner or later covered by the media. It is possible as a result, with some extra information, to assemble a readable collection revealing the sequence of events, to extract the important concepts, and to see the turning points. Several industrial or corporate crises in recent years have been particularly well documented. Well worth reading are *States of Emergency* by P. Lagadec (1990) and case studies about major technical failures such as the Amoco Cadiz oil spill, the first major civil nuclear power crisis at Three Mile Island, the Bhopal disaster, the fire at a Sandoz warehouse in Basle, and pollution of the Rhine; the incredible story of the disappearance in Europe in 1982 of forty-two barrels of toxic material contaminated with dioxin following the July 10, 1976, accident at a Givaudan-Hoffmann-La Roche group factory at Seveso in Italy and the crisis in 1979 in which safety concerns kept all DC10s worldwide on the ground following an American Airlines plane crash during take-off from Chicago.

This educational method also makes it possible, based on examples, to demonstrate how important the initial communication by the company affected by the incident can be. These observations can then be used to take the analysis further, developing it into a real matrix for reading the dynamics of a crisis, deducing practical lessons on the procedures and facilities that help to cope and on the working methods needed to react in an appropriate way.

II. SETTING UP A CRISIS UNIT

In the event of a technical accident, each high-risk industrial site should be able to call on a team of managers in a position to implement, effectively, an emergency plan established for this kind of incident. The same is true for managers of a business, subsidiary, or corporate head office. In the case of a serious incident, they will have to set up what is generally called an emergency control station or a crisis unit. Experience shows that in reality many companies and public or private organizations still only have a very vague and incomplete approach to this subject. Sometimes a procedure exists but it is often old and theoretical and has never been put to the test in an exercise.

The role of training for a crisis is first to require critical reading of planned emergency procedures, if they exist. Are they usable in practice? Will the crisis unit planned on paper be able to meet quickly, even if it is outside working hours? Above all, when should the unit be convened and will it then really be able to play its role to the full?

It is essential to understand that a crisis unit is, by definition, an operational entity. It is to be designed as such and not to be put together like a management committee. The aim is to react very quickly and implement a whole range of concrete actions on various fronts, both in a strategic manner and as quickly as possible. That is of course impossible if the planned entity consists from the start of too many decision-making levels and if the responsibilities and tasks of each member of the unit are not clearly defined, and even more so if the designated managers have no practice. Working in a crisis unit cannot be improvised whatever the individual skills. Allowance also has to be made for the complexity of crises and for the major roles played by stress and media pressure. That is why the members of a crisis unit need to be familiarized, through exercises, with the company procedures, planned premises, communications equipment, and working methods to be used under such conditions.

III.   SIMULATION EXERCISES

A.   *Crisis Drills Represent the Decisive Training Stage*

The emergency procedure needs to be tested by an established team to determine whether it is appropriate and operational. However detailed the work may appear on paper, being faced with the need to implement procedures in a concrete situation always reveals breakdowns and major shortfalls that cannot be predicted in advance, most of which turn out to be easy to remedy. The benefit of these drills always becomes apparent to the participants.

The principle behind a simulation is to offer the company's crisis unit a fictitious initial incident requiring urgent operational actions, e.g., controlling a technical accident, evacuation for health reasons, or product batch recall, along with a range of internal and external communication steps. This initial situation is chosen following analysis of the likely potential risks for the site or business concerned. Just as in real-life situations, the case will include incomplete information, uncertainties, and even errors. It will be designed to develop over time with surges and interventions by various players who enter the game, telephone, and ask questions, such as families, local residents, the media, government authorities, local representatives, business relations, employees, and customers. The unit will therefore have to develop both an operational and a communications strategy.

B.   *Several Types of Drills Are Possible Depending on Objectives*

The incident can be entirely virtual, in which case the drill is based on a group of role-playing games with a flow of written or oral information. Alternatively, the drill might consist of real operations such as forwarding equipment or evacuating supposed wounded along with communications activities all performed at the same time.

In any event, the scenario must always be designed according to clearly defined objectives. It is important to know exactly what resources and people need to be tested and/or proven. To encourage immediate support from participants, it is essential that the initial incident be perfectly credible. In particular, all technical aspects of the scenario need to be developed with the collaboration of experienced specialists. In the case of an accident, it is best if these technical matters are authenticated by reference to the actual scene itself. To achieve the greatest possible realism, it is useful to base the story on lessons learned from the experience of real events. The roles of involved outsiders should also be devised carefully to achieve undisputed credibility. This realism is important since it will help to obtain reliable observations on the emotional component of a crisis unit's operation. *Experience shows that behavior observed in a well-designed simulation does not differ fundamentally from that in a real incident.* In general terms, simulations help to generate very precise diagnoses of the improvements required. In industries facing major technical risks, most large industrial groups such as Elf and Rhône-Poulenc have been committed for several years to training programs that include regular crisis drills. Many international companies and public bodies would reportedly also be interested in training their teams.

IV.   PREPARING FOR CRISIS PREVENTION AND AVOIDANCE

A.   *From Crisis Unit to Crisis Watch*

It is essential for a company to know how to manage a crisis should one arise, but it is preferable to know how to avoid one. This just slightly academic statement would be of little interest if experience had not shown that a large number of crises in all business sectors are actually avoidable. In addition, the term *crisis* may be abusively applied these days to just about any serious situation, but it is nonetheless true that not all serious incidents, whether accident or conflict, turn into real crises. In other words, a crisis does not develop by accident or fate and it is perfectly possible to act, that is to prevent it, with action best taken upstream.

Analysis of a large number of crises reveals that there were often advance signals. These warnings failed to find any place in an effective internal information channel or managers did not pay sufficient attention to them. Whatever the reasons, the result was a failure to assess the true potential risk. Alternatively, when the risk was quite clearly identified, management of it may have been delayed or blocked as a result of differing attitudes and considerations, most often short-term savings.

For this reason many crises occur after maturing for several days, weeks, or months.

To avoid such dramatic developments a company that already has a crisis unit may take the next step toward a preventive approach by organizing a crisis watch. In practice this means putting together a small committee of a few managers whose task is to identify and assess quickly any warning signal that might arise. This group has clear authority from the company's highest levels and its opinions are passed back to the same levels for decisions to be taken.

Such a crisis watch unit's organization and operating methods are quite simple once the substantial managerial and financial benefit is understood and once a motivated team that can implement it has been put together. The first principle is that it must be multidisciplinary. The crisis watch unit should include one manager from each operational or functional department to act as the access point for any warning signals. Their task is to watch for potential warning signs or risk, even in the medium to long term, in the stream of daily information, either from outside the company in the form of the media, seminars, business meetings, proposed laws, or complaints, or from inside in the form of accident reports, meetings, or memos. This may be a matter involving a company product either directly or indirectly, a subject affecting the company's business, or a general theme that might involve it. Any new information of this kind acquired by a member of the unit should be passed on quickly and systematically to the other unit members. A risk that might appear very low to one manager may be perceived as very serious by another because of the extra information he or she possesses. When potential risk is considered possible, probable, of concern, or even alarming in the short term, unit members must meet as quickly as possible to discuss and move on to the next stage. This consists of assessing the real risk and, if necessary, informing senior management and initiating preventive measures. Risks identified as having no potential to develop in the short term are assessed at monthly meetings.

Setting up a crisis watch unit in this way helps the company to be forearmed against the so-called *Tartar Steppe syndrome* (from the famous Dino Buzzatti novel), i.e., "waiting for a crisis which never comes and, when it does happen, [being surprised because] attention has long since dropped off" (Lagadec 1993b).

B.　Risk Audits

When considering crisis prevention, companies are advised to assign the resources needed to intervene upstream, at least in those areas with particular potential risk. Well-conducted audits give precise results and excellent reliability. A product risk audit, for example, will have four stages:

　　1.　Identification Consists of Three Basic Aspects:

- Review of risks already identified.　These generally account for 70 to 80 percent of all risks, but information is often scattered across various departments.
- Review of each product's history.　This includes problems that have already occurred relating to the product itself, but problems that might have affected both the product category and competing products must also be considered.
- A systematic stage-by-stage-approach from raw material or component supply to marketing.　Each potential risk level needs to be reviewed, including all levels of subcontractor involvement. The auditors' experience, i.e., their knowledge of risk areas and situations, is a determining factor. The best method is to work in pairs with one internal and one external auditor.

　　2.　Assessment.　For each risk identified, the potential risk level can be assessed using the scenario method.

　　3.　Setting Priorities.　A hierarchy of identified risks is established using two criteria: potential seriousness and probability of occurrence. This makes it possible to separate unacceptable from acceptable risks. It is important, however, to understand that a risk considered acceptable from a technical point of view may be considered unacceptable in the public eye.

　　4.　Preventive Action.　Preventive action ranging from technical intervention to reinforcing user information, via adopting new procedures and/or new standards, may then follow logically.

Conclusion

We believe categorically that *communicating in crisis* "does not aim to cover unacceptable deficiencies in safety, [political and] social equilibrium [nor that] its objective is to attempt to implement stopgap measures, [to minimize or even hide responsibility]. . . . It is not [therefore] a collection of tactical recipes secretly shared by a select few." [1]

Learning crisis expertise, behavior, and communication skills should be a top corporate priority for decision-makers. Experience shows that well-managed crisis communication can encourage the best possible processing of dramatic events when they risk having a terrible impact on the natural environment or on society, and as a result can avoid considerable human, social, and economic cost.

NOTE

1. Bracketed phrases are author's addition to original quotation from P. Lagadec.

References

Bolzinger, A. 1982. "Le concept clinique de crise." *Bulletin de psychologie* 35(355): 475–80.

Campion-Vincent, V., and J.-B. Renard. 1992. *Légendes urbaines: Rumeurs d'aujour-d'hui.* Paris: Payot.

Dab, W. 1993. *La décision en santé publique.* Rennes: ENSP.

Delanglade, S. 1996. *L'Express,* 14 November.

Delumeau, J., and Y. Lequin. 1987. *Les malheurs des temps: Histoire des fléaux et des calamités en France.* Paris: Larousse.

Dormont, D., O. Bletry, and F.-F. Delfraissy. 1989. *Les 365 nouvelles maladies.* Paris: Médecines-Sciences, Flammarion.

Drucker, J. 1977. In *Médias, Pouvoirs et Démocratie.* Paris: Institut International de Géopolitique.

Filizzola, G., and G. Lopez. 1995. *Victimes et victimologie.* "Que sais-je." Paris: Presse Universitaires de France.

Hirsch, M., P. Duneton, P. Baralon, and F. Noiville. 1996. *L'affolante histoire de la "vache folle."* Paris: Balland.

Janis, I. 1982. *Groupthink: Psychological Studies of Policy Decisions and Fiascoes.* New York: Houghton Mifflin.

Kapferer, J.-N. 1987–1990. *Rumeurs.* Paris: Éd. Le Seuil.

Kauffmann, S. 1996. *Le Monde,* 12 April.

Lagadec, P. 1981. *La civilisation du risque.* Paris: Éd. Le Seuil.

Lagadec, P. 1982. *Major Technological Risk: An Assessment of Industrial Disasters.* Oxford: Pergamon.

Lagadec, P. 1990. *States of Emergency, Technological Failures and Social Destabilisation.* London: Butterworth-Heinemann.

Lagadec, P. 1993a. *Preventing Chaos in a Crisis: Strategy for Prevention, Control and Damage Limitation.* London: McGraw-Hill.

Lagadec, P. 1993b. *Apprendre à gérer les crises.* Paris: Les Éd. d'Organisation.

Lagadec, P. 1995. *Cellules de crise.* Paris: Les Éd. d'Organisation.

Lemaître, F. 1996. *Le Monde,* 13 November.

Mayle, F. 1996. *Amiante. Le dossier de l'air contaminé.* Paris: Éd. Le Pré-aux-Clercs.

Morelle, A. 1996. *La défaite de la santé publique.* Paris: Éd. Flammarion.

Morin, E. 1976. "Pour une crisologie." *Communications* 25.

Mucchielli, A. 1993. *Communication interne et management de la crise.* Paris: Les Éd. d'Organisation.

Ogrizek, M. 1993. "Environnement et communication de crise." In *Environnement et communication.* Rennes: Apogée.

Ogrizek, M., J.-M. Guillery, and C. Mirabaud. 1996. "La communication médicale de crise." In *La communication médicale.* "Que sais-je." Paris: Presse Universitaires de France.

Scanlon, J. 1975. "Crisis Communications in Canada." In *Communications in Canadian Society.* Toronto: B. D. Singes.

Scanlon, J. 1982. "Crisis Communications: The Ever-Present Gremlins." Emergency Communications Unit. Presentation at Congress Comcon '82, Arnprior, Ontario, 26 May.

Shibutani, T. 1996. "A Sociological Study of Rumor." In *Improvise News.* Indianapolis: Bobbs Merrill.

Soulez Larivière, D. 1993. *Du cirque médiatico-judiciaire et des moyens d'en sortir,* Essai politique. Paris: Éd. Le Seuil.

Walther, E. 1994. "Dictionnaire des 'Affaires' ("Dictionary of Scandals"). *Capital* (December).